Volume B

FUNDAMENTALS OF
ENGLISH
GRAMMAR

Second Edition

Volume B

FUNDAMENTALS OF
ENGLISH
GRAMMAR
Second Edition

Betty Schrampfer Azar

Longman

Library of Congress Cataloging-in-Publication Data

Azar, Betty Schrampfer, 1941–
  Fundamentals of English grammar / Betty Schrampfer Azar. — 2nd
ed.
    p. cm.
  Includes index
  ISBN 0-13-327552-3 (v. A : pbk.)
  ISBN 0-13-347139-X (v. B : pbk.)
  1. English language—Textbooks for foreign speakers. 2. English
language—Grammar—1950– I. Title.
PE1128.A965 1992b   92-7657
428.2′4—dc20   CIP

Publisher: *Tina B. Carver*
Managing editor, production: *Sylvia Moore*
Editorial/production supervision: *Janet Johnston*
Prepress buyer: *Ray Keating*
Manufacturing buyer: *Lori Bulwin*
Scheduler: *Leslie Coward*
Illustrations: *Don Martinetti*
Cover supervisor: *Karen Salzbach*
Cover designer: *Joel Mitnick Design*
Interior designer: *Ros Herion Freese*
Page makeup: *Mary Fitzgerald*

© 1992 by Prentice Hall Regents
A Pearson Education Company
Pearson Education 10 Bank Street, White Plains, NY 10606

Printed in the United States of America

        14 15 - CRS - 02 01

ISBN 0-13-338278-8

ISBN 0-13-327552-3 {VOL.A}

ISBN 0-13-347139-X {VOL.B}

To my sister,
JO

Contents

Preface to the Second Edition

Fundamentals of English Grammar remains a developmental skills text for mid-level students of English as a second or foreign language. It focuses on key structures and provides ample opportunities for practice through extensive and varied exercises. While focusing on grammar, it promotes the development of all language skills.

The chief difference in the second edition of *Fundamentals of English Grammar* is the inclusion of additional grammar areas that are important at the intermediate level. The principal additions deal with personal pronouns; forms of *other*; connecting ideas with coordinating and subordinating conjunctions, including the use of commas and periods; and comparisons. Other short units have also been included: for example, the use of *must* to make logical conclusions; expressing immediate future with *be about to*; nonspecific vs. specific pronouns (e.g., *May I have one* vs. *May I have it*); uncompleted infinitives; and using a gerund after a preposition. This edition seeks to fill in gaps in an intermediate grammar syllabus. Not every class will cover every unit, but the second edition makes a broad table of contents available. Other changes in the second edition are directed toward clarifying the structure presentations in the charts and improving the exercises.

Another significant difference in the second edition lies in the support material: a workbook and a teacher's guide.

The workbook provides independent study opportunities in the form of Selfstudy Practices (with the answers given). It also provides Guided Study Practices (no answers given) for additional classwork, homework, and individualized instruction as the teacher sees the need.

The teacher's guide contains presentation suggestions; specific techniques for handling the varied types of exercises; background grammar notes; item notes on cultural content, vocabulary, and structure usage; problems to anticipate; suggestions for oral and written student-centered activities; and answers to the exercises.

Acknowledgments

Many people have parts in the work I do as a writer. They make my work possible and enjoyable.

I wish especially to thank Donald Azar, Tina Carver, Barbara Matthies, and Janet Johnston.

In addition, I wish to thank Joy Edwards, R. T. Steltz, Susan Abbott, Jonni Reed, Ralph Hastings, Gordon Adams, Frank Sullivan, Sylvia Moore, Andy Martin, Efrain Rojas, Gil Muller, Noel Carter, Dennis Hogan, Anne Riddick, Mary Vaughn, Don Martinetti, Gordon Johnson, Rick Spencer, Eric Bredenberg, Ed Stanford, Rick Essig, Jack Ross, David Haines, Sally Howard, Ray Keating, Ed Perez, Roger Olsen, Judy Winn-Bell Olsen, Martin Tenney, Wayne Spohr, Norman Harris, Terry Jennings, Jerry Smith, Bruce Kennan, Connie Hernandez, Amelia Azar, and Chelsea Parker.

Special appreciation is due the seven reviewers who marked up copies of the first edition to guide the revisions: Gari Browning, Arline Burgmeier, Linda Misja, Larry Robinson, Luis Sanchez, Grace Tanaka, and Cheryl Youtsey. Their insights were invaluable.

Last, I want to thank my amazing parents. Both are retired educators in their late 80s. My father wrote reams of ideas for exercise entries, for this revision and for the workbook. My mother input the entire text of the first edition so that I had it available for revision on disk. How can I thank them enough? Maybe by saying it in print—Thanks, Mom and Dad. Thank you very, very much.

CHAPTER 9
Connecting Ideas

☐ **EXERCISE 1—PREVIEW:** Add PUNCTUATION (commas and periods) and CAPITAL
LETTERS if necessary. Do not change or add any words. Identify SUBJECTS (S)
and VERBS (V).

1. Butterflies are insects all insects have six legs.

        S   **V**   **S**   **V**

  → ***Butterflies are insects. All insects have six legs.***

2. Ants and butterflies are insects.

3. Ants butterflies cockroaches bees and flies are insects.

4. Butterflies and bees are insects spiders are different from insects.

5. Spiders have eight legs so they are not called insects.

6. Most insects have wings but spiders do not.

7. Bees are valuable to us they pollinate crops and provide us with honey.

8. Some insects bite us and carry diseases.

9. Insects can cause us trouble they bite us carry diseases and eat our
food.

10. Insects are essential to life on earth the plants and animals on earth
could not live without them insects may bother us but we have to share
this planet with them.

11. We have to share the earth with insects because they are essential to
plant and animal life.

12. Because insects are necessary to life on earth it is important to know
about them.

9-1 CONNECTING IDEAS WITH *AND*

When *and* connects only two items within a sentence, NO COMMAS are used. When *and* connects three or more items in a series in a sentence, commas are used.

(a) I saw a *cat* **and** a *mouse*.	In (a): **and** connects two nouns: *cat* + *mouse* = NO COMMAS
(b) I saw a *cat*, a *mouse*, **and** a *rat*. I saw a *cat*, a *mouse*, a *rat*, **and** a *dog*.	In (b): **and** connects three or more nouns, so commas are used.★
(c) I *opened* the door **and** *walked* into the room.	In (c): NO COMMAS are used because **and** connects only two verbs (*opened* + *walked*).
(d) I *opened* the door, *walked* into the room, **and** *sat* down at my desk.	In (d): Commas are used because **and** connects three verbs (*opened* + *walked* + *sat*).
(e) Their flag is *green* **and** *black*.	In (e): **and** connects two adjectives (NO COMMAS).
(f) Their flag is *green*, *black*, **and** *yellow*.	In (f): **and** connects three adjectives (commas).

When *and* connects two sentences, a comma is usually used.

(g) I opened the door. She opened the window. (h) INCORRECT: I opened the door, she opened the window.	In (g): Two complete sentences (also called independent clauses) are separated by a period, NOT a comma.★★ (h) is incorrect because it has a comma between the two independent clauses.
(i) I opened the door, **and** she opened the window.	In (i): When **and** connects two independent clauses, a comma is usually used.

★In a series of three or more items, the comma before **and** is optional.
   ALSO CORRECT: *I saw a cat, a mouse and a rat.*

★★Notice that a capital letter (''S'' not ''s'') follows the period in (g). The first word in a new sentence is capitalized. See Chart 4-14 for more information about capitalization. Also note that a *period* is called a *full stop* in British English.

□ **EXERCISE 2:** Add COMMAS where appropriate.

1. My aunt puts milk and sugar in her tea. (*no commas*)

2. My aunt puts milk sugar and lemon in her tea.

→ ***My aunt puts milk, sugar, and lemon in her tea.***

3. Tom ate a sandwich and drank a glass of milk.

4. Tom made a sandwich poured a glass of milk and sat down to eat his lunch.

5. Cats and dogs are animals.

6. Cows goats and horses are farm animals.

7. Giraffes anteaters tigers and kangaroos are wild animals.

8. The river is wide and deep.

9. The river is wide deep and dangerous.

10. Doctors save lives and relieve suffering.

11. Doctors save lives relieve suffering and cure diseases.

12. The restaurant served a five-course dinner: soup fish entreé salad and dessert.

13. I had fish and a salad for dinner last night.

14. The children played games sang songs drew pictures and had a piece of birthday cake.

15. An invitation should include your name address the date the time the purpose of the party and any special activities such as swimming or dancing.

☐ **EXERCISE 3:** Add COMMAS and PERIODS where appropriate. CAPITALIZE as necessary.

1. I talked he listened.

   → ***I talked. He listened.***

2. I talked and he listened.

   → ***I talked, and he listened.*** *

3. I talked to Ryan about his school grades and he listened to me carefully.

   → ***I talked to Ryan about his school grades, and he listened to me carefully.***

4. I talked to Ryan about his grades he listened carefully and promised to improve them.

   → ***I talked to Ryan about his school grades. He listened carefully and promised to improve them.***

5. The river rose it flooded the towns in the valley.

6. The river rose and flooded the towns in the valley.

7. The river rose and it flooded the towns in the valley.

8. The river rose it flooded the towns and farms in the valley.

9. The river and streams rose they flooded the towns and farms in the valley.

---

*Sometimes the comma is omitted when **and** connects two very short independent clauses. ALSO CORRECT: *I talked and he listened.* In longer sentences, the comma is important and usual.

10. Rome is an Italian city it has a mild climate and many interesting attractions.

11. You should visit Rome its climate is mild and there are many interesting attractions.

12. The principal metals used to make coins are gold silver copper and nickel.

13. Coins are made of metal and last for a long time paper money has a short life span.

14. Collecting stamps can teach a youngster about some of the famous people and events in a country's history.

15. The United States is bounded by two oceans and two countries the oceans are the Pacific to the west and the Atlantic to the east and the countries are Canada to the north and Mexico to the south.

9-2 CONNECTING IDEAS WITH *BUT* AND *OR*

(a) I *went* to bed *but couldn't sleep.* (b) Is a lemon *sweet or sour?* (c) Did you order *coffee, tea, or milk?*	*And*, *but*, and *or* are called "conjunctions." *But* and *or* are used in the same ways as *and* (see 9-1). Notice: Only (c) uses commas.
(d) I dropped the vase, *but* it didn't break. (e) Do we have class on Monday, *or* is Monday a holiday?	Commas are usually used when *but* or *or* connects two complete sentences.* (*I dropped the vase* = a complete sentence.) (*it didn't break* = a complete sentence.)

*Sometimes with *but*, a period is used instead of a comma.
ALSO POSSIBLE: *I dropped the vase. But it didn't break.*

☐ **EXERCISE 4:** Add *and*, *but*, or *or*. Add COMMAS if necessary.

1. I washed my shirt __*, but*__ it didn't get clean.

2. Would you like some water ____*or*____ some fruit juice?

3. I washed my face **,** brushed my teeth __*, and*__ took a shower.

4. I invited the Carters to dinner _____ they couldn't come.

5. You can have chicken fish _____ beef for dinner.

6. The flight attendants served dinner _____ I didn't eat.

7. I was hungry _____ didn't eat on the plane. The food didn't look appetizing.

8. Jennifer wore boots jeans a long-sleeved shirt _____ gloves when she worked in her garden.

9. Golf _____ tennis are popular sports.

10. Sara is a good tennis player _____ she's never played golf.

11. Which would you prefer? Would you like to play tennis _____ golf Saturday morning?

12. Who called whom? Did Bob call you _____ did you call Bob?

☐ **EXERCISE 5:** Add COMMAS, PERIODS, and CAPITAL LETTERS as appropriate.

1. Cats are mammals turtles are reptiles.

    → ***Cats are mammals. Turtles are reptiles.***

2. Cats are mammals but turtles are reptiles.

3. Cows are farm animals but zebras are wild animals.

4. Cows and horses are farm animals but zebras and giraffes are wild animals.

5. Cows and horses are farm animals zebras giraffes and lions are wild animals.

6. Cars use roads trains run on tracks.

7. Cars use roads but trains run on tracks.

8. Cars buses and trucks use roads but trains run on tracks.

9. Most vegetables grow above the ground but some are roots and grow under the ground corn beans and cabbage grow above the ground but carrots and beets grow under the ground.

10. A good office has modern equipment such as computers intercoms and copying machines but the most important part of a good office is the people who work there.

9-3 CONNECTING IDEAS WITH *SO*

(a) The room was dark, *so* I turned on a light.	*So* can be used as a conjunction. It is preceded by a comma. It connects the ideas in two independent clauses. *So* expresses **results**:
(b) I didn't study, *so* I failed the exam.	cause: *the room was dark* result: *I turned on a light*

☐ **EXERCISE 6:** Add *so* or *but*. Add COMMAS where appropriate.

1. It began to rain _____**, so**_____ I opened my umbrella.

2. It began to rain _____**, but**_____ I didn't have my umbrella with me.

3. I didn't have an umbrella _____ I got wet.

4. I didn't have an umbrella _____ I didn't get wet because I was wearing my raincoat.

5. The water was cold _____ I didn't go swimming.

6. The water was cold _____ I went swimming anyway.

7. Scott's directions to his apartment weren't clear _____ George got lost.

8. The directions weren't clear _____ I found Scott's apartment anyway.

9. My friend lied to me _____ I still like and trust her.

10. My friend lied to me _____ I don't trust her anymore.

☐ **EXERCISE 7:** Add COMMAS, PERIODS, and CAPITAL LETTERS as appropriate. Don't change any of the words or the order of the words.

1. James has a cold he needs to rest and drink plenty of fluids so he should go to bed and drink water fruit juices or soda pop he needs to sleep a lot so he shouldn't drink fluids with caffeine such as tea or coffee.

   → *James has a cold. He needs to rest and drink plenty of fluids, so he should go to bed and drink water, fruit juice, and soda pop. He needs to sleep a lot, so he shouldn't drink fluids with caffeine such as tea and coffee.*

2. My friend and I were tired so we went home early we had wanted to stay until the end of the game but it got too late for us both of us had to get up early in the morning and go to our jobs.

3. The normal pulse for an adult is between 60 and 80 beats per minute but exercise nervousness excitement and a fever will all make a pulse faster the normal pulse for a child is around 80 to 90.

4. Many famous explorers throughout history set out on their hazardous journeys in search of gold silver jewels or other treasures but some explorers wanted only to discover information about their world.

5. Edward Fox was a park ranger for thirty-five years during that time, he was hit by lightning eight times the lightning never killed him but it severely burned his skin and damaged his hearing.

6. The Indian Ocean is bordered on four sides by the continents of Africa Asia Australia and Antarctica some of the important ports are Aden Bombay Calcutta and Rangoon.

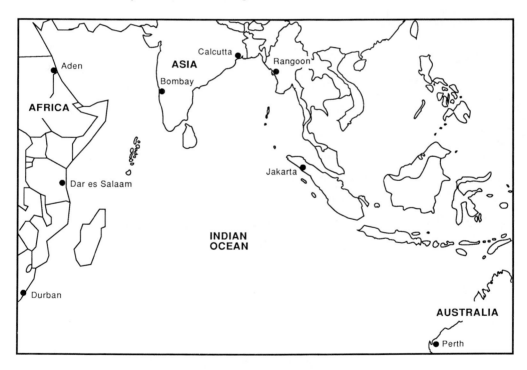

7. The Indian Ocean has many fish and shellfish but it has less commercial fishing than the Atlantic or the Pacific the climate of the Indian Ocean is tropical so fish spoil quickly out of the water it is difficult and expensive for commercial fishing boats to keep fish fresh.

9-4 USING AUXILIARY VERBS AFTER *BUT* AND *AND*

(a) I *don't like coffee*, **but** my husband *does*. (b) I *like tea*, **but** my husband *doesn't*. (c) I *won't be here tomorrow*, **but** Sue *will*. (d) I *'ve seen that movie*, **but** Joe *hasn't*. (e) He *isn't here*, **but** she *is*.*	After **but** and **and**, often a main verb is not repeated. Instead, only an auxiliary verb is used. The auxiliary is a substitute for the main verb phrase. The auxiliary after **but** and **and** has the same tense or modal as the main verb. In (a): *does = likes coffee*. The auxiliary *does* (simple present) is the substitute for the main verb phrase (simple present).
(f) I *don't like coffee*, **and** Ed *doesn't* either. (g) I *like tea*, **and** Kate *does* too. (h) I *won't be here*, **and** he *won't* either. (i) I *'ve seen that movie*, **and** Pat *has* too. (j) He *isn't here*, **and** Anna *isn't* either.	Notice in the examples: *negative* + **but** + *affirmative* *affirmative* + **but** + *negative* *negative* + **and** + *negative* *affirmative* + **and** + *affirmative*

*A verb is not contracted with a pronoun at the end of a sentence after **but** and **and**:
    CORRECT: . . . *but she is.*
    INCORRECT: . . . *but she's.*

□ **EXERCISE 8:** Practice using auxiliary verbs after **but** and **and**.

1. Dan didn't study for the test, but Amy _____**did**_____ .

2. Alice doesn't come to class every day, but Julie _____.

3. Jack went to the movie last night, but I _____.

4. I don't live in the dorm, but Rob and Jim _____.

5. Rob lives in the dorm, and Jim _____ too.

6. I don't live in the dorm, and Carol _____ either.

7. My roommate was at home last night, but I _____.

8. Ted isn't here today, but Alex _____.

9. Ted isn't here today, and Linda _____ either.

10. The teacher is listening to the tape, and the students _____ too.

11. Susan won't be at the meeting tonight, but I _____.

12. Susan isn't going to go to the meeting tonight, but I _____.

13. I'll be there, but she _____.

14. I'll be there, and Mike _____ too.

15. I can speak French, and my wife _____ too.

16. I haven't finished my work yet, but Erica _____.

17. I didn't finish my work last night, but Erica _____.

18. Jane would like a cup of coffee, and I _____ too.

☐ **EXERCISE 9:** Complete the sentences by using the names of your classmates and appropriate auxiliary verbs.

1. _____*Kunio*_____ has a mustache, but _____*Kutaiba doesn't*_____.

2. _____*Maria*_____ doesn't have brown eyes, but _____*Boris does*_____.

3. _____ isn't in class today, but _____.

4. _____ is here today, but _____.

5. _____ can speak Spanish, but _____.

6. _____ can't speak Japanese, but _____.

7. _____ stayed home last night, but _____.

8. _____ didn't come to class yesterday, but _____.

9. _____ will be at home tonight, but _____.

10. _____ won't be on time, but _____.

11. _____ isn't wearing jeans today, but _____.

12. _____ has long hair, but _____.

13. _____ has lived here for a long time, but _____.

14. _____ lives in an apartment, but _____.

15. _____ doesn't have a car, but _____.

☐ **EXERCISE 10:** Complete the sentences by using the names of your classmates. Add *too* (if the auxiliary verb is affirmative) or *either* (if the auxiliary verb is negative) to the end of the sentences.

1. _____*Carlos*_____ has a pen with blue ink, and _____*Yoko does too*_____.

2. _____*Ali*_____ doesn't speak Chinese, and _*Roberto doesn't either*_.

3. _____ isn't married, and _____.

4. _____ sits in the same seat every day, and _____.

5. _____ is wearing jeans today, and _____.

6. _____ walked to class today, and _____.

7. _____ was in class yesterday, and _____.

8. _____ didn't call me last night, and _____.

9. _____ isn't married, and _____.

10. _____ comes to class every day, and _____.

11. _____ has brown eyes, and _____.

12. _____ has been here for over a month, and _____.

13. _____ doesn't have a beard, and _____.

14. _____ can't speak Arabic, and _____.

15. _____ will be in class tomorrow, and _____.

9-5 USING *AND + TOO, SO, EITHER, NEITHER*

AND . . . TOO AND SO . . .	(a) Sue likes milk, AND + S + *aux* + TOO and Tom does too. (b) Sue likes milk, AND + SO + *aux* + S and so does Tom.	(a) and (b) have the same meaning. Notice in (b): After *and so* . . ., the auxiliary verb (*aux*) comes before the subject (S).
AND . . . EITHER AND NEITHER . . .	(c) Mary doesn't like milk, AND + S + *aux* + EITHER and John doesn't either. (d) Mary doesn't like milk, AND + NEITHER + *aux* + S and neither does John.	(c) and (d) have the same meaning. Notice in (d): After *and neither* . . . , the auxiliary verb comes before the subject. Notice in (c): A negative auxiliary verb is used with *and . . . either*. In (d): An affirmative auxiliary verb is used with *and neither* . . . .
(e) A: I'm hungry. B: **I am too**. (g) A: I don't like hot dogs. B: **I don't either**.	(f) A: I'm hungry. B: **So am I**. (h) A: I don't like hot dogs. B: **Neither do I**.	**And** is usually not used when there are two speakers. (e) and (f) have the same meaning. (g) and (h) have the same meaning.
(i) A: I'm hungry. B: **Me too**. (*informal*)	(j) A: I don't like hot dogs. B: **Me neither**. (*informal*)	**Me too** and **me neither** are often used in informal spoken English.

☐ **EXERCISE 11:** Complete the sentences by using the word in italics and an appropriate auxiliary.

1. Tom   Jack has a mustache, and so _____ ***does Tom*** _____.

               Jack has a mustache, and _____ ***Tom does*** _____ too.

2. Brian   Alex doesn't have a mustache, and neither _____.

               Alex doesn't have a mustache, and _____ either.

3. *I*   Sara was at home last night, and so _____.

Sara was at home last night, and _____ too.

4. *Oregon*   California is on the West Coast, and so _____.

California is on the West Coast, and _____ too.

5. *Jean*   I went to a movie last night, and so _____.

I went to a movie last night, and _____ too.

6. *Jason*   I didn't study last night, and neither _____.

I didn't study last night, and _____ either.

7. *Dick*   Jim can't speak Arabic, and neither _____.

Jim can't speak Arabic, and _____ either.

8. *Laura*   I like to go to science fiction movies, and so _____.

I like to go to science fiction movies, and _____ too.

9. *Alice*   I don't like horror movies, and neither _____.

I don't like horror movies, and _____ either.

10. *porpoises*   Whales are mammals, and so _____.

Whales are mammals, and _____ too.

BLUE WHALE

PORPOISE

11. *I*   Karen hasn't seen that movie yet, and neither _____.

Karen hasn't seen that movie yet, and _____ either.

12. *my brother*   I have a car, and so _____.

I have a car, and _____ too.

13. *Erin*   Rob won't join us for lunch, and neither _____.

Rob won't join us for lunch, and _____ either.

☐ **EXERCISE 12:** Complete the sentences by using the names of your classmates and appropriate auxiliaries.

1. _____*Maria*_____ wasn't in class yesterday, and neither _**was Jin Won**_.

2. _____ is wearing slacks today, and so _____.

3. _____ lives in an apartment, and so _____.

4. _____ can't speak Chinese, and neither _____.

5. _____ stayed home and studied, and so _____.

6. _____ doesn't have a mustache, and neither _____.

7. _____ will be in class tomorrow, and so _____.

8. _____ isn't married, and neither _____.

9. _____ has dimples, and so _____.

10. _____ has been in class all week, and so _____.

☐ **EXERCISE 13:** Complete the dialogues by agreeing with SPEAKER A's idea. Use *so* or *neither*. Use *I*.

1. A: I'm tired.

   B: _____*So am I.*_____

2. A: I didn't enjoy the movie last night.

   B: _____*Neither did I.*_____

3. A: I've never been in France.*

   B: _____*Neither have I.*_____

4. A: I always have a cup of coffee in the morning.

   B: _____

5. A: I don't feel like going to class today.

   B: _____

6. A: I've never been in Brazil.

   B: _____

7. A: I need to go to the bank today.

   B: _____

_____
*****Never** makes a sentence negative.

8. A: I studied last night.

   B: _____

9. A: I didn't eat breakfast this morning.

   B: _____

10. A: I should stay home and study tonight.

    B: _____

11. A: I have a roommate.

    B: _____

12. A: I've never visited Vancouver, British Columbia.

    B: _____

13. A: I don't have a car.

    B: _____

14. A: I have to go downtown this afternoon.

    B: _____

15. A: I can't speak Hungarian.

    B: _____

16. A: But I can speak English.

    B: _____

□ **EXERCISE 14—ORAL (BOOKS CLOSED):** Respond to the statements by using *so* or *neither*.

Example: Los Angeles is in California.
Response: So is (San Francisco).

1. (. . .) speaks (*language*).
2. (. . .) doesn't speak (*language*).
3. (. . .) is wearing (*jeans*) today.
4. (. . .) isn't wearing (*jeans*) today.
5. (. . .) came to class yesterday.
6. (. . .) has been in (*this city*) for (*time*).
7. (. . .) can't speak (*language*).
8. (*A city*) is in (*this state/province*).
9. The United States is in North America.
10. (Niagara Falls) is a famous landmark.
11. Ants are insects.
12. A bicycle has two wheels.
13. Mercury is a planet.
14. Snakes don't have legs.
15. Chickens lay eggs.
16. Copper is a metal.
17. Coffee contains caffeine.
18. The sun is a source of energy.
19. Pencils aren't expensive.
20. Paper burns.

9-6 CONNECTING IDEAS WITH *BECAUSE*

(a) He drank water *because* he was thirsty.	***Because*** expresses a cause; it gives a reason. Why did he drink water? Reason: he was thirsty.
(b) MAIN CLAUSE: *He drank water.*	A main clause is a complete sentence: *He drank water.* = a complete sentence.
(c) ADVERB CLAUSE: *because he was thirsty*	An adverb clause is NOT a complete sentence: *because he was thirsty* = NOT a complete sentence. ***Because*** introduces an adverb clause: ***because*** + *subject* + *verb* = *an adverb clause.*
main clause adverb clause (d) ⌐He drank water⌐ ⌐*because he was thirsty.*⌐ (no comma)	An adverb clause is connected to a main clause, as in (d) and (e).* In (d): **main clause + *no* comma + adverb clause.** In (e): **adverb clause + comma + main clause.**
adverb clause main clause (e) ⌐*Because he was thirsty,*⌐ ⌐he drank water.⌐ (comma)	(d) and (e) have exactly the same meaning.
(f) INCORRECT: He drank water. Because he was thirsty.	(f) is incorrect: *because he was thirsty* cannot stand alone as a sentence that starts with a capital letter and ends with a period. It has to be connected to a main clause as in (d) and (e).

*See Chart 2-8 for a discussion of other adverb clauses. "Time clauses" are adverb clauses that are introduced by *when, after, before,* and *while.*

☐ **EXERCISE 15:** Combine each pair of sentences in two different orders. Use ***because***.

1. We didn't have class. The teacher was absent.

   → ***We didn't have class because the teacher was absent.***

   → ***Because the teacher was absent, we didn't have class.***

2. The children were hungry. There was no food in the house.

3. The bridge is closed. We can't drive to the other side of the river.

4. My car didn't start. The battery was dead.

5. Debbie woke up in the morning with a sore throat. She had cheered loudly at the basketball game.

☐ **EXERCISE 16:** Complete the sentences with *so* or *because*. Add COMMAS where appropriate. CAPITALIZE as necessary.

1. a. He was hungry _____, **so**_____ he ate a sandwich.

   b. _____**Because**_____ he was hungry **,** he ate a sandwich.

   c. He ate a sandwich _____**because**_____ he was hungry.

2. a. _____ my sister was tired she went to bed.

   b. My sister went to bed _____ she was tired.

   c. My sister was tired _____ she went to bed.

3. a. _____ human beings have opposable thumbs they can easily pick things up and hold them.

   b. Human beings have opposable thumbs _____ they can easily pick things up and hold them.

   c. Human beings can easily pick things up and hold them _____ they have opposable thumbs.

4. a. Schoolchildren can usually identify Italy easily on a world map _____ it is shaped like a boot.

   b. _____ Italy has the distinctive shape of a boot schoolchildren can usually identify it easily.

   c. Italy has the distinctive shape of a boot _____ schoolchildren can usually identify it easily on a map.

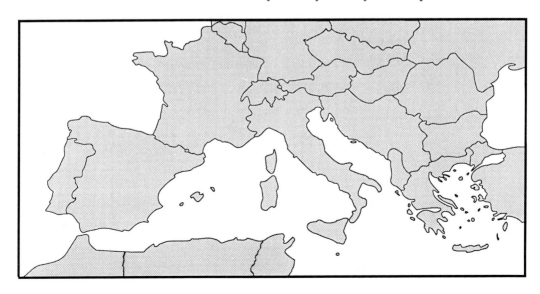

□ **EXERCISE 17:** Add COMMAS, PERIODS, and CAPITAL LETTERS as appropriate. Don't change any of the words or the order of the words.

1. Jim was hot he sat in the shade.

2. Jim was hot and tired he sat in the shade.

3. Jim was hot and tired so he sat in the shade.

4. Jim was hot tired and thirsty.

5. Because he was hot Jim sat in the shade.

6. Because he was hot and thirsty Jim drank some tea.

7. Because he was hot and thirsty Jim sat in the shade and drank some tea.

8. Because they were hot and thirsty Jim and Susan sat in the shade and drank tea.

9. Jim and Susan sat in the shade and drank tea because they were hot and thirsty.

10. Jim sat in the shade drank tea and fanned himself because he was hot tired and thirsty.

11. Because Jim was hot he stayed under the shade of the tree but Susan went back to work.

12. Mules are domestic animals they are the offspring of a horse and a donkey mules are called ''beasts of burden'' because they can work hard and carry heavy loads.

13. Because mules are strong they can work under harsh conditions but they need proper care.

14. A wolf howls because it is separated from its pack or its pup has died.

15. Ann had been looking for an apartment for two weeks yesterday she went to look at an apartment on Fifth Avenue she rented it because it was in good condition and had a nice view of the city she was glad to find a new apartment.

16. The word ''matter'' is a chemical term matter is anything that has weight this book your finger water a rock air and the sun are all examples of matter radio waves and heat are not matter because they do not have weight happiness daydreams and fear have no weight and are not matter.

9-7 CONNECTING IDEAS WITH *EVEN THOUGH/ALTHOUGH*

(a) ***Even though*** I was hungry, I did not eat.
  I did not eat ***even though*** I was hungry.
(b) ***Although*** I was hungry, I did not eat.
  I did not eat ***although*** I was hungry.
	Even though and *although* introduce an adverb clause.
	
	(a) and (b) have the same meaning. They mean:
	  I was hungry, but I did not eat.

COMPARE: (c) *Because* I was hungry, *I ate.* (d) *Even though* I was hungry, *I did not eat.*	*Because* expresses an expected result. *Even though/although* expresses an unexpected or opposite result.

☐ **EXERCISE 18:** Complete the sentences by using *even though* or *because*.

1. _____**Even though**_____ the weather is cold, Rick isn't wearing a coat.

2. _____ the weather is cold, Ben is wearing a coat.

3. _____ Tim is fairly tall, he can't reach the ceiling.

4. _____ Matt is very tall, he can reach the ceiling.

5. _____ Dan isn't as tall as Matt, he can't reach the ceiling.

6. _____ Nick isn't tall, he can reach the ceiling by standing on a chair.

TIM   MATT   DAN   NICK

7. _____ Jane was sad, she smiled.

8. _____ Jane was sad, she cried.

9. _____ her street is dangerous, Carol doesn't go out alone after dark.

10. _____ his street is dangerous, Steve often goes out alone after dark.

11. Tony sings at weddings _____ he has a good voice.

12. George sings loudly _____ he can't carry a tune.

13. Louie didn't iron his shirt _____ it was wrinkled.

14. Eric ironed his shirt _____ it was wrinkled.

15. Kate went to a dentist _____ she had a toothache.

16. Colette didn't go to a dentist _____ she had a toothache.

17. Jennifer went to a dentist _____ she didn't have a toothache. She just wanted a checkup.

18. I would like to raise tropical fish _____ it's difficult to maintain a fish tank in good condition.

19. The baby shoved the pills into his mouth _____ they looked like candy. _____ he ingested several pills, he didn't get sick. Today many pill bottles have child-proof caps _____ children may think pills are candy and poison themselves.

20. _____ our friends live on an island, it is easy to get there _____ there is a bridge from the mainland.

□ **EXERCISE 19—ORAL (BOOKS CLOSED):** Answer "yes" or "no," as you wish. Answer in a complete sentence using either **because** or **even though**. Change the wording as you wish.

Example: Last night you were tired. Did you go to bed early?

Response: Yes, I went to bed early because I was tired. OR:
Yes, because I was tired, I went to bed before nine. OR:
No, I didn't go to bed early even though I was really sleepy. OR:
No, even though I was really tired, I didn't go to bed until after midnight.

1. Last night you were tired. Did you stay up late?
2. You are thirsty. Do you want (a glass of water)?
3. You're hungry. Do you want (a candy bar)?
4. Vegetables are good for you. Do you eat a lot of them?
5. Space exploration is exciting. Would you like to be an astronaut?
6. Guns are dangerous. Do you want to own one?
7. (A local restaurant) is expensive/inexpensive. Do you eat there?
8. (A local delicacy) is/are expensive. Do you buy it/them?
9. The (name of a local) river is/isn't polluted. Do you want to swim in it?
10. Who (in this room) can't swim? Do you want to go to (the beach/the swimming pool) with (. . .) and me this afternoon?
11. Who loves to go swimming? Do you want to go to (the beach/the swimming pool) with (. . .) and me this afternoon?
12. What are the winters like here? Do you like living here in winter?
13. (A recent movie) has had good reviews. Do you want to see it?
14. Are you a good artist? Do you want to draw a picture of me on the board?
15. Where is your family? Are you going to go there (over the next holiday)?

□ **EXERCISE 20—WRITTEN:** Complete the following with your own words. Pay attention to proper punctuation.

1. I like our classroom even though . . . .
2. I like my (*apartment, dorm room, etc.*) because . . . .
3. . . . even though I don't . . . .
4. . . . because I don't . . . .
5. Even though I didn't . . . , ...
6. Because I didn't . . . , ...
7. . . . because . . . salty.
8. . . . even though . . . very hot.
9. Because . . . , the world is a better place.
10. Even though . . . , I can usually communicate what I mean.
11. People put up fences because . . . .
12. Even though the government has built large apartment complexes, ...
13. Even though most people in the world desire peace, ...
14. . . . because life is hard.
15. Even though . . . , life has many joys.
16. . . . because . . . .
17. Even though . . . , ...
18. Because . . . , I . . . , but . . . .

□ **EXERCISE 21—ERROR ANALYSIS:** Correct the errors in the following sentences. Pay special attention to punctuation.

1. Even though I was sick, but I went to work.

   → *Even though I was sick, I went to work.*

   → *I was sick, but I went to work.*

2. Gold silver and copper. They are metals.

3. The students crowded around the bulletin board. Because their grades were posted there.

4. I'd like a cup of coffee, and so does my friend.

5. I like coffee, but my friend does.

6. Even I am very exhausted, I didn't stop working until after midnight last night.

7. The teacher went too the meeting, and too of the students did two.

8. Although I like chocolate, but I can't eat it because I'm allergic to it.

9. Many tourists visit my country. Warm weather all year. Many interesting landmarks.

10. Because the weather in my country is warm and comfortable all year so many tourists visit it in the winter.

11. I like to eat raw eggs for breakfast and everybody else in my family too.

12. A hardware store sells tools and nails and plumbing supplies and paint and etc.★

13. Because the war broke out in late September we had to cancel our October trip even though we already had our passports visas airplane tickets and hotel reservations.

14. Many of us experience stress on our jobs my job is stressful because my workplace is not pleasant or comfortable it is noisy hot and dirty even though I try to do my best my boss is unhappy with my work and always gives me bad performance reports I need to find another job.

★***Etc.*** is an abbreviation of the Latin *et cetera*. It means "and other things of a similar nature." The word ***and*** is NOT used in front of ***etc***.
   INCORRECT: *The farmer raises cows, sheep, goats,* ***chickens, and etc.***
   INCORRECT: *The farmer raises cows, sheep, goats,* ***and chickens, etc.***
   Also, notice the spelling: *etc.* NOT *ect.*

9-8 PHRASAL VERBS (SEPARABLE)

(a) We **put off** our trip.	In (a): **put off** = *a phrasal verb.*★ *A phrasal verb* = a verb and a particle that together have a special meaning. For example, **put off** means "postpone." *A particle* = a preposition (e.g., *off, on*) or an adverb (e.g., *away, back*) that is used in a phrasal verb.
(b) We *put off* our trip. (c) We *put our trip* off. (d) I *turned on* the light. (e) I *turned the light* on.	Many phrasal verbs are **separable.**★★ In other words, a NOUN can either follow or come between (separate) the verb and the particle. (b) and (c) have the same meaning. (d) and (e) have the same meaning.
(f) We *put it off*. (g) I *turned it on*.	If a phrasal verb is **separable**, the PRONOUN always comes between the verb and the particle; the pronoun never follows the particle. INCORRECT: *We put off it.* INCORRECT: *I turned on it.*

SOME COMMON PHRASAL VERBS (SEPARABLE)

figure out........*find the solution to a problem*
hand in.........*give homework, test papers, etc., to a teacher*
hand out ....*give something to this person, then that person, then another person, etc.*
look up.........*look for information in a dictionary, a telephone directory, an encyclopedia, etc.*
make up.........*invent a story*
pick up.........*lift*
put down ....*stop holding or carrying*
put off..........*postpone*
put on..........*put clothes on one's body*
take off.........*remove clothes from one's body*
throw away⎫
throw out ⎬.....*put in the trash, discard*
turn off.........*stop a machine or a light*
turn on.........*start a machine or a light*
wake up.........*stop sleeping*
write down ......*write a note on a piece of paper*

★*Phrasal verbs are also called* two-word verbs *and* three-word verbs.
★★Some phrasal verbs are **nonseparable**. Chart 9-9 will discuss nonseparable phrasal verbs. See Appendix 2 for a list of phrasal verbs.

☐ **EXERCISE 22:** Complete the sentences with the following particles: *away, down, in, off, on, out, up.*

1. Before I left home this morning, I put _____ my coat.

2. When I got to class this morning, I took my coat _____.

3. The students handed their homework _____.

4. Johnny made a story _____. He didn't tell the truth.

5. The weather was bad, so we put _____ the picnic until next week.

6. Alice looked a word _____ in her dictionary.

7. Alice wrote the definition _____.

8. My roommate is messy. He never picks _____ his clothes.

9. The teacher handed the test papers _____ at the beginning of the class period.

10. A strange noise woke _____ the children in the middle of the night.

11. When some friends came to visit, Chris stopped watching TV. He turned the television set _____.

12. It was dark when I got home last night, so I turned the lights _____.

13. Peggy finally figured _____ the answer to the arithmetic problem.

14. When I was walking through the airport, my arms got tired. So I put my suitcases _____ for a minute and rested.

15. I threw _____ yesterday's newspaper.

□ **EXERCISE 23:** Complete the sentences with pronouns and particles.

1. A: Did you postpone your trip to Puerto Rico?

   B: Yes, we did. We put _____**it off**_____ until next summer.

2. A: Is Pat's phone number 322–4454 or 322–5545?

   B: I don't remember. You'd better look _____. The telephone directory is in the kitchen.

3. A: Is Mary still asleep?

   B: Yes. I'd better wake _____. She has a class at nine.

4. A: Do you want to keep these newspapers?

   B: No. Throw _____.

5. A: I'm hot. This sweater is too heavy.

   B: Why don't you take _____?

6. A: Is that story true?

   B: No. I made _____.

7. A: When does the teacher want our compositions?

   B: We have to hand _____ tomorrow.

8. A: I made an appointment with Dr. Armstrong for three o'clock next Thursday.

   B: You'd better write _____ so you won't forget.

9. A: Do you know the answer to this problem?

   B: No. I can't figure _____.

10. A: Johnny, you're too heavy for me to carry. I have to put _____.

    B: Okay, Mommy.

11. A: Where are the letters I put on the kitchen table?

    B: I picked _____ and took them to the post office.

12. A: How does this tape recorder work?

    B: Push this button to turn _____, and push that button to turn _____.

13. A: I have some papers for the class. Ali, would you please hand _____ for me?

    B: I'd be happy to.

14. A: Timmy, here's your hat. Put _____ before you go out. It's cold outside.

    B: Okay, Dad.

9-9 PHRASAL VERBS (NONSEPARABLE)

(a) I *ran into Bob* at the bank yesterday. (b) I saw Bob yesterday. I *ran into him* at the bank.	If a phrasal verb is **nonseparable**, a noun or pronoun follows (never precedes) the particle. INCORRECT: *I ran Bob into at the bank.* INCORRECT: *I ran him into at the bank.*

SOME COMMON PHRASAL VERBS (NONSEPARABLE)

call on .... *ask to speak in class*
get over .... *recover from an illness*
run into .... *meet by chance*
get on .... *enter* ⎫
get off .... *leave* ⎬ *a bus, an airplane, a train, a subway, a bicycle*
get in .... *enter* ⎫
get out of ...... *leave* ⎬ *a car, a taxi*

□ **EXERCISE 24:** Complete the sentences with particles. Discuss the meaning of the phrasal verbs in the sentences.

1. When I raised my hand in class, the teacher called _____ me.

2. While I was walking down the street, I ran _____ an old friend.

3. Fred feels okay today. He got _____ his cold.

4. Last week I flew from Chicago to Miami. I got _____ the plane in Chicago. I got _____ the plane in Miami.

5. Sally took a taxi to the airport. She got _____ the taxi in front of her apartment building. She got _____ the taxi at the airport.

6. I take the bus to school every day. I get _____ the bus at the corner of First Street and Sunset Boulevard. I get _____ the bus just a block away from the classroom building.

□ **EXERCISE 25—ORAL (BOOKS CLOSED):** Complete the sentences.

Example: Yesterday I cleaned my closet. I found an old pair of shoes that I don't ever wear anymore. I didn't keep the shoes. I threw . . . .
Response: them away/out.

1. The teacher gave us some important information in class yesterday. I didn't want to forget it, so I wrote . . . .

2. When I raised my hand in class, the teacher called . . . .

3. I was carrying a suitcase, but it was too heavy, so I put . . . .

4. I didn't know the meaning of a word, so I looked . . . .

5. I was sleepy last night, so I didn't finish my homework. I put . . . .

6. It was dark when I got home, so I turned . . . .

7. (. . .) isn't wearing his/her hat right now. When s/he got to class, s/he took . . . .

8. My pen just fell on the floor. Could you please pick . . . ?

9. I saw (. . .) at a concert last night. I was surprised when I ran . . . .

10. When you finish using a stove, you should always be careful to turn . . . .

11. When I finished my test, I handed . . . .

12. Is (. . .) sleeping?! Would you please wake . . . ?

13. What's the answer to this problem? Have you figured . . . ?

14. I don't need this piece of paper anymore. I'm going to throw . . . .

15. I had the flu last week, but now I'm okay. I got . . . .
16. I told a story that wasn't true. I made . . . .
17. Name some means of transportation that you get on.
18. Name some that you get in.
19. Name some that you get off.
20. Name some that you get out of.
21. Name some things that you turn on.
22. Name some things that you turn off.

CHAPTER 10
Gerunds and Infinitives

10-1 GERUNDS AND INFINITIVES: INTRODUCTION

(a) I enjoy **music.** *(noun)*	**S V O** *I enjoy* **something**. (*something* = the object of the verb.) The object of a verb is usually a noun or pronoun, as in (a). The object of a verb can also be a gerund. A gerund is *the -ing form of a verb.** It is used as a noun.
(b) I enjoy ***listening*** to music. *(gerund)*	
(c) I enjoy ***listening to music.*** *(gerund phrase)*	In (b): ***listening*** is a gerund. It is the object of the verb ***enjoy***.
(d) I want **a sandwich.** *(noun)*	**S V O** *I want* **something**. (*something* = the object of the verb.) In (d): The object of the verb is a noun (*a sandwich*). The object of a verb can also be an infinitive. An infinitive is **to** + *the simple form of a verb*.
(e) I want ***to eat*** a sandwich. *(infinitive)*	
(f) I want ***to eat*** a sandwich. *(infinitive phrase)*	In (e): ***to eat*** is an infinitive. It is the object of the verb ***want***.
(g) I *enjoy* **going** to the beach.	Some verbs (e.g., *enjoy*) are followed by gerunds. (See 10-2.)
(h) Ted *wants* **to go** to the beach.	Some verbs (e.g., *want*) are followed by infinitives. (See 10-4.)
(i) It *began* **raining**. It *began* **to rain**.	Some verbs (e.g., *begin*) are followed by either gerunds or infinitives. (See 10-5.)

*The **-ing** form of a verb can be used as a present participle:
   *I **am listening** to the teacher right now.* (**listening** = a present participle, used in the present progressive)
  The -ing form of a verb can be used as a gerund:
   *I **enjoy listening** to music.* (**listening** = a gerund, used as the object of the verb **enjoy**)

10-2 VERB + GERUND

COMMON VERBS FOLLOWED BY GERUNDS		Gerunds are used as the objects of the verbs in the list. The list also contains phrasal verbs (e.g., *put off*) that are followed by gerunds.
enjoy	(a) I *enjoy working* in my garden.	
finish	(b) Bob *finished studying* at midnight.	
*stop**	(c) It *stopped raining* a few minutes ago.	These verbs are NOT followed by infinitives.* For example:
quit	(d) David *quit smoking*.	INCORRECT: *I enjoy to work.*
mind	(e) Would you *mind opening* the window?	INCORRECT: *Bob finished to study.* INCORRECT: *I'm thinking to go to Hawaii.*
postpone	(f) I *postponed doing* my homework.	
put off	(g) I *put off doing* my homework.	
keep	(h) *Keep working*. Don't stop.	
keep on	(i) *Keep on working*. Don't stop.	
consider	(j) I*'m considering going* to Hawaii.	
think about	(k) I*'m thinking about going* to Hawaii.	
discuss	(l) They *discussed getting* a new car.	See Chart 2-5 for the spelling of *-ing* verb forms.
talk about	(m) They *talked about getting* a new car.	
(n) I considered *not going* to class.		Negative form: *not* + *gerund*.

*The object following *stop* is a gerund, NOT an infinitive. INCORRECT: *It stopped to rain.*
But in a special circumstance, *stop* can be followed by an infinitive of purpose: *in order to* (see Chart 10-11). *While I was walking down the hall, I dropped my pen.* **I stopped to pick** *it up.* = I ***stopped walking in order to pick*** *it up.*

☐ **EXERCISE 1:** Complete the sentences by using gerunds. Add a preposition after the gerund if necessary.

1. It was cold and rainy yesterday, so we postponed __*going to/visiting*__
   the botanical gardens.

2. The Porter's house is too small. They're considering __*buying/*__
   __*moving into/renting*__ a bigger house.

3. We discussed _____ Colorado for our vacation.

4. When Martha finished _____ the floor, she dusted
   the furniture.

5. Sometimes students put off _____ their homework.

6. We had a blizzard yesterday, but it finally stopped _____
   around ten P.M.

7. I quit _____ comic books when I was twelve years
   old.

8. I'm thinking about _____ a biology course next semester.

9. Beth doesn't like her job. She's talking about _____ a different job.

10. I enjoy _____ sports.

11. I'm considering _____ New York City.

12. A: Are you listening to me?

    B: Yes. Keep _____. I'm listening.

13. A: Do you want to take a break?

    B: No. I'm not tired yet. Let's keep on _____ for another hour or so.

14. A: Would you mind _____ the window?

    B: Not at all. I'd be glad to.

□ **EXERCISE 2:** Complete the sentences in the dialogues. Use the expressions in the list or your own words. Be sure to use a gerund in each sentence.

buy a new car	*rain*
do my homework	*read a good book*
do things	*repeat that*
get a Toyota	*smoke*
go to the zoo on Saturday	*tap your fingernails on the table*
help him	*try*

1. A: Would you like to go for a walk?

   B: Has it stopped ___*raining*_____?

   A: Yes.

   B: Let's go.

2. A: I've been having a lot of trouble with my old Honda the last couple of months. It's slowly falling apart. I'm thinking about _____

   _____.

   B: Do you think you'll get another Honda?

   A: No. I'm considering _____.

3. A: What do you usually do in your free time in the evening?

   B: I enjoy _____.

4. A: Good news! I feel great. I don't cough any more, and I don't run out of breath when I walk up a hill.

   B: Oh?

   A: I quit _____.

   B: That's wonderful!

5. A: I've been working on this math problem for the last half hour, and I still don't understand it.

   B: Well, don't give up. Keep _____. If at first you don't succeed, try, try again.

6. A: Are you a procrastinator?

   B: A what?

   A: A procrastinator. That's someone who always postpones _____

   _____.

   B: Oh. Well, sometimes I put off _____.

7. A: What are you doing?

   B: I'm helping Teddy with his homework.

   A: When you finish _____, could you help me in the kitchen?

   B: Sure.

8. A: Could you please stop doing that?

   B: Doing what?

   A: Stop _____. It's driving me crazy.

9. A: Do you have any plans for this weekend?

   B: Henry and I talked about _____.

10. A: I didn't understand what you said. Would you mind _____

    _____?

    B: Of course not. I said, "Three free trees."

10-3 GO + -ING

(a) **Did** you **go shopping** yesterday?
 (b) I **went swimming** last week.
 (c) Bob **hasn't gone fishing** in years.
	Go is followed by a gerund in certain idiomatic expressions about activities.
	 Notice: There is no **to** between **go** and the gerund.
	     INCORRECT: *Did you go to shopping?*
	     CORRECT: *Did you go shopping?*

COMMON EXPRESSIONS WITH *GO + -ING*

go boating	*go hiking*	*go sightseeing*
go bowling	*go jogging*	*go skating*
go camping	*go running*	*go (water) skiing*
go dancing	*go sailing*	*go skydiving*
go fishing	*go (window) shopping*	*go swimming*

☐ **EXERCISE 3—ORAL:** Answer the questions. Use the expressions with *go + -ing* in Chart 10-3.

    1. Ann often goes to the beach. She spends hours in the water. What does she like to do?
      → *She likes to go swimming.*

2. Nancy and Frank like to spend the whole day on a lake with poles in their hands. What do they like to do?

3. Last summer Adam went to a national park. He slept in a tent and cooked his food over a fire. What did Adam do last summer?

4. Tim likes to go to stores and buy things. What does he like to do?

5. Laura takes good care of her health. She runs a couple of miles every day. What does Laura do every day? (*Note: There are two possible responses.*)

6. On weekends in the winter, Fred and Jean sometimes drive to a resort in the mountains. They like to race down the side of a mountain in the snow. What do they like to do?

7. Joe is a nature lover. He likes to take long walks in the woods. What does Joe like to do?

8. Sara prefers indoor sports. She goes to a place where she rolls a thirteen-pound ball at some wooden pins. What does Sara often do?

9. Liz and Greg know all the latest dances. What do they probably do a lot?

10. The Taylors are going to go to a little lake near their house tomorrow. The lake is completely frozen now that it's winter. The ice is smooth. What are the Taylors going to do tomorrow?

11. Barbara and Alex live near the ocean. When there's a strong wind, they like to spend the whole day in their sailboat. What do they like to do?

12. Tourists often get on buses that take them to see interesting places in an area. What do tourists do on buses?

13. Colette and Ben like to jump out of airplanes. They don't open their parachutes until the last minute. What do they like to do?

14. What do you like to do for exercise and fun?

10-4 VERB + INFINITIVE

(a) Tom **offered to lend** me some money. (b) I've **decided to buy** a new car.	Some verbs are followed by an infinitive: AN INFINITIVE = **to** + *the simple form of a verb.*
(c) I've **decided not to keep** my old car.	Negative form: **not** + *infinitive.*

COMMON VERBS FOLLOWED BY INFINITIVES

want	*hope*	*decide*	*seem*	*learn (how)*
need	*expect*	*promise*	*appear*	*try*
would like	*plan*	*offer*	*pretend*	
would love	*intend*	*agree*		*(can't) afford*
	mean	*refuse*	*forget*	*(can't) wait*

☐ **EXERCISE 4:** Complete the sentences by using INFINITIVES. Add a PREPOSITION after the infinitive if necessary.

1. I'm planning ___***to go to/to visit/to drive to***___ Chicago next week.

2. I've decided _____ a new apartment.

3. Jack promised not _____ late for the wedding.

4. I forgot _____ some milk when I went to the grocery store.

5. I would like _____ the Grand Canyon.

6. My husband and I would love _____ Arizona.

7. I need _____ my homework tonight.

8. What time do you expect _____ Chicago?

9. I want _____ a ball game on TV after dinner tonight.

10. You seem _____ in a good mood today.

11. Susie appeared _____ asleep, but she wasn't. She was only pretending.

12. Susie pretended _____ asleep. She pretended not _____ me when I spoke to her.

13. The Millers can't afford _____ a house.

14. George is only seven, but he intends _____ a doctor when he grows up.

15. My friend offered _____ me a little money.

16. Tommy doesn't like peas. He refuses _____ them.

17. My wife and I wanted to do different things this weekend. Finally, I agreed _____ a movie with her Saturday, and she agreed _____ the football game with me on Sunday.

18. I hope _____ all of my courses this term. So far my grades have been pretty good.

19. I try _____ class on time every day.

20. I can't wait _____ my family again! It's been a long time!

21. I'm sorry. I didn't mean _____ you.

22. I learned (how) _____ when I was around six or seven.

10-5 VERB + GERUND OR INFINITIVE

(a) It *began* **to rain**. (b) It *began* **raining**.	Some verbs are followed by either an infinitive or a gerund. Usually there is no difference in meaning. (a) and (b) have the same meaning.

COMMON VERBS FOLLOWED BY EITHER A GERUND OR AN INFINITIVE		
begin	*like*★	*hate*
start	*love*★	*can't stand*
continue		

★COMPARE: ***Like*** and ***love*** can be followed by either a gerund or an infinitive:
I like going/to go to movies. I love playing/to play chess.

Would like and ***would love*** are followed by infinitives:
I would like to go to a movie tonight. I'd love to play a game of chess right now.

☐ **EXERCISE 5—ORAL:** Use the given words to make sentences with GERUNDS and INFINITIVES.

1. start + snow around midnight

   → *It started snowing around midnight. It started to snow around midnight.*

2. continue + work even though everyone else stopped

3. like + listen to music while I'm studying

4. love + go to baseball games

5. hate + talk to pushy salespeople

6. can't stand + wait in lines for a long time

☐ **EXERCISE 6:** Complete the sentences with the INFINITIVE or GERUND form of the words in parentheses.

1. I need (*study*) _____ **to study** _____ tonight.

2. I enjoy (*cook*) _____ **cooking** _____ gourmet meals.

3. Ellen started (*talk*) _____ **to talk/talking** _____ about her problem.

4. Bud and Sally have decided (*get*) _____ married.

5. We finished (*eat*) _____ around seven.

6. Are you planning (*take*) _____ a vacation this year?

7. I like (*meet*) _____ new people.

8. The Wilsons went (camp) _____ in Yellowstone National Park last summer.

9. My roommate offered (help) _____ me with my English.

10. I'd just begun (watch) _____ a movie on TV when the phone rang.

11. Please stop (crack) _____ your knuckles!

12. Did you remember (feed) _____ the cat this morning?

13. I won't be late. I promise (be) _____ on time.

14. I'm considering (move) _____ to a new apartment.

15. What time do you expect (arrive) _____ in Denver?

16. Some children hate (go) _____ to school.

17. I forgot (lock) _____ the door when I left my apartment this morning.

18. I don't mind (live) _____ with four roommates.

19. Don't put off (write) _____ your composition until the last minute.

20. Ken had to quit (jog) _____ because he hurt his knee.

21. The company will continue (hire) _____ new employees as long as new production orders keep (come) _____ in.

22. That's not what I meant! I meant (say) _____ just the opposite.

23. I want (go) _____ (shop) _____ this afternoon.

24. Alex seems (want) _____ (go) _____ (sail) _____ this weekend.

□ **EXERCISE 7:** Complete the sentences with the INFINITIVE or GERUND form of the words in parentheses.

1. Cindy intends (go) _____ to graduate school next year.

2. Pierre can't afford (buy) _____ a new car.

3. Janice is thinking about (look) _____ for a new job.

4. My boss refused (*give*) _____ me a raise, so I quit.

5. Mr. Carter continued (*read*) _____ his book even though the children were making a lot of noise.

6. Shhh. My roommate is trying (*take*) _____ a nap.

7. Dick appears (*have*) _____ a lot of money.

8. Eric agreed (*meet*) _____ us at the restaurant at seven.

9. Have you discussed (*change*) _____ your major with your academic advisor?

10. I haven't heard from Stacy in a long time. I keep (*hope*) _____ that I'll get a letter from her soon.

11. My wife can't stand (*sleep*) _____ in a room with all of the windows closed.

12. Sam's tomato crop always failed. Finally he quit (*try*) _____ (*grow*) _____ tomatoes in his garden.

13. Would you like (*go*) _____ (*dance*) _____ tonight?

14. The Knickerbockers talked about (*build*) _____ a new house.

15. Children like (*play*) _____ make-believe games. Yesterday Jason pretended (*be*) _____ a doctor, and Bobby pretended (*be*) _____ a patient.

16. My cousin offered (*take*) _____ me to the airport.

17. I'm planning (*go*) _____ (*shop*) _____ tomorrow.

18. Would you mind (*pass*) _____ this note to Joanna? Thanks.

19. Tim expects (*go*) _____ (*fish*) _____ this weekend.

20. When Tommy broke his toy, he started (*cry*) _____.

21. Jerry likes (*go*) _____ to professional conferences.

22. Would you like (*go*) _____ to Sharon's house next Saturday?

23. I expect (be) _____ in class tomorrow.

24. I enjoy (teach) _____.

25. I enjoy (be) _____ a teacher.

□ **EXERCISE 8—ORAL:** Pair up with another student.

STUDENT A: Read the cues. Your book is open.
STUDENT B: Complete the sentences with either ***to go*** or ***going*** + *the name of a place.*

Example:
STUDENT A: I expect . . . .
STUDENT B: to go (to Mack's Bar and Grill for dinner tonight).
STUDENT A: I like . . . .
STUDENT B: to go (to Hawaii). OR: . . . going (to Hawaii).

Switch roles halfway through: STUDENT A *becomes* STUDENT B *and vice versa.*

1. I expect . . . .
2. I like . . . .
3. I would like . . . .
4. I enjoy . . . .
5. I'd love . . . .
6. I promised . . . .
7. I can't stand . . . .
8. I intend . . . .
9. I am thinking about . . . .
10. Are you considering . . . .
11. I refuse . . . .
12. I've always wanted . . . .
13. I can't afford . . . .
14. I'd enjoy . . . .
15. I don't need . . . .
16. I'm going to try . . . .
17. I hate . . . .
18. I love . . . .
19. My friend and I discussed . . . .
20. I've decided . . . .
21. My friend and I postponed . . . .
22. Sometimes I put off . . . .
23. Yesterday I forgot . . . .
24. I can't wait . . . .
25. My friend and I agreed . . . .
26. Would you mind . . . .

□ **EXERCISE 9:** Complete the sentences with a form of the words in parentheses.

1. I enjoy (get) _____ up early in the morning.

2. I enjoy (watch) _____ the sunrise.

3. I enjoy (get) _____ up early in the morning and (watch) _____ the sunrise.

4. I enjoy (get) _____ up early in the morning, (watch) _____ the sunrise, and (listen) _____ to the birds.

5. I want (stay) _____ home tonight.

6. I want (*relax*) _____ tonight.

7. I want (*stay*) _____ home and (*relax*)* _____ tonight.

8. I want (*stay*) _____ home, (*relax*) _____ , and (*go*) _____ to bed early tonight.

9. Mr. and Mrs. Brown are thinking about (*sell*) _____ their old house and (*buy*) _____ a new one.

10. Kathy plans (*move*) _____ to New York City, (*find*) _____ a job, and (*start*) _____ a new life.

□ **EXERCISE 10:** Complete the sentences with a form of the words in parentheses.

1. Have you finished (*paint*) _____ your apartment yet?

2. Steve needs (*go*) _____ to the shopping mall tomorrow and (*buy*) _____ winter clothes.

3. Don't forget (*call*) _____ the dentist's office this afternoon.

4. Do you enjoy (*go*) _____ to an expensive restaurant and (*have*) _____ a gourmet dinner?

5. Most nonsmokers can't stand (*be*) _____ in a smoke-filled room.

6. Let's postpone (*go*) _____ abroad until the political situation improves.

7. The children promised (*stop*) _____ (*make*) _____ so much noise.

8. How do you expect (*pass*) _____ your courses if you don't study?

9. Kevin is thinking about (*quit*) _____ his job and (*go*) _____ back to school.

_____

*When infinitives are connected by **and**, it is not necessary to repeat **to**:
    *I need **to stay** home **and** (to) **study** tonight.*

10. Linda plans (*leave*) _____ for Chicago on Tuesday and (*return*) _____ on Friday.

11. I often put off (*wash*) _____ the dinner dishes until the next morning.

12. Shhh. I'm trying (*concentrate*) _____. I'm doing a problem for my accounting class, and I can't afford (*make*) _____ any mistakes.

13. I'm sleepy. I'd like (*go*) _____ home and (*take*) _____ a nap.

14. When are you going to start (*do*) _____ the research for your term paper?

15. Why did Marcia refuse (*help*) _____ us?

16. Don't forget (*unplug*) _____ the coffee pot, (*turn off*) _____ all the lights, and (*lock*) _____ the door before you leave for work this morning.

17. Sometimes when I'm listening to someone who is speaking English very fast, I nod my head and pretend (*understand*) _____.

18. After Isabel got a speeding ticket and had to pay a big fine, she decided (*stop*) _____ (*drive*) _____ over the speed limit on interstate highways.

19. Khalid tries (*learn*) _____ at least 25 new words every day.

20. I considered (*drive*) _____ to Minneapolis. Finally I decided (*fly*) _____.

21. Our teacher agreed (*postpone*) _____ the test until Friday.

22. I've been trying (*reach*) _____ Carol on the phone for the last three days, but she's never at home. I intend (*keep*) _____ (*try*) _____ until I finally get her.

☐ **EXERCISE 11—ORAL (BOOKS CLOSED):** Make sentences from the given words. Use *I*. Use any tense.

> *Example:* *want* and *go*
> *Response:* I want to go (to New York City next week).

1. *plan* and *go*	16. *promise* and *come*
2. *consider* and *go*	17. *finish* and *study*
3. *offer* and *lend*	18. *would mind* and *help*
4. *like* and *visit*	19. *hope* and *go*
5. *enjoy* and *read*	20. *think about* and *go*
6. *intend* and *get up*	21. *quit* and *drink*
7. *decide* and *get*	22. *expect* and *stay*
8. *seem* and *be*	23. *stop* and *eat*
9. *put off* and *write*	24. *refuse* and *lend*
10. *forget* and *go*	25. *agree* and *lend*
11. *can't afford* and *buy*	26. *postpone* and *go*
12. *try* and *learn*	27. *begin* and *study*
13. *need* and *learn*	28. *continue* and *walk*
14. *would love* and *take*	29. *talk about* and *go*
15. *would like* and *go* and *swim*	30. *keep* and *try* and *improve*

10-6   UNCOMPLETED INFINITIVES

(a) I've never met Rita, but *I'd like **to***. (b) INCORRECT: I've never met Rita, but I'd like. (c) INCORRECT: I've never met Rita, but I'd like it. (d) INCORRECT: I've never met Rita, but I'd like to do.	In (a): *I'd like **to*** = an uncompleted infinitive; *I'd like **to meet Rita*** = the understood completion. An infinitive phrase is not completed following ***to*** when the meaning is clearly understood to repeat the idea that came immediately before. Uncompleted infinitives follow the verbs in Charts 10-4 and 10-5.
(e) I don't want to leave, but *I have **to***. (f) Sam doesn't go to school here, but *he used **to***.	Uncompleted infinitives are also common with these auxiliaries: *have to, be going to, used to,* and *ought to*.

☐ **EXERCISE 12:** Complete the sentences with the words in parentheses. Use any appropriate tense. Discuss the understood meaning of the uncompleted infinitives.

> 1. A: Why didn't you go to the concert?
>   B: I (*want, not*) _____ **didn't want to** _____.

2. I haven't written my parents yet this week, but I (*intend*)

   _____.

3. A: Did Jane enjoy the play?

   B: She (*seem*) _____.

4. I'd like to buy fresh flowers for my desk every day, but I can't (*afford*)

   _____.

5. I've never eaten at that restaurant, but I (*would like*)

   _____.

6. A: Want to go to the jazz festival with us tomorrow night?

   B: I (*would love*) _____!

7. A: Are you going to the historical society meeting?

   B: Yes, I (*plan*) _____. And you?

8. Oh! I'm sorry I closed the door in your face! I (*mean, not*)

   _____!

9. I don't play with toys anymore, but I (*use*) _____.

10. A: Have you called Jennifer yet?

    B: That's the fourth time you've asked me. I (*be going*)

    _____! I (*be going*) _____!

    Don't be a nag!

11. Tina doesn't feel like going to the meeting, but she (*have*)

    _____.

12. A: Are you planning to go to the market?

    B: No, but I suppose I (*ought*) _____.

10-7 PREPOSITION + GERUND

(a) Kate *insisted **on coming*** with us. (b) We*'re excited **about going*** to Tahiti. (c) I *apologized **for being*** late.	A preposition is followed by a gerund, not an infinitive. In (a): preposition (*on*) + gerund (*coming*)

☐ **EXERCISE 13:** Complete the sentences. Use PREPOSITIONS* and GERUNDS.

1. Bill interrupted me. He apologized ____**for**____ that.

   → Bill apologized _____**for interrupting**_____ me.

2. I like to learn about other countries and cultures. I'm interested _____ that.

   → I'm interested _____ about other countries and cultures.

3. I helped Ann. She thanked me _____ that.

   → Ann thanked me _____ her.

4. Jessica wanted to walk to work. She insisted _____ that.

   → We offered Jessica a ride, but she insisted _____ to work.

5. Nick lost my car keys. I forgave him _____ that.

   → I forgave Nick _____ my car keys when he borrowed my car.

6. Sara wanted to go to a movie, but James didn't want to. They argued _____ that.

   → Sara and James argued _____ to a movie.

7. Jake cuts his own hair. Instead _____ that, he should go to a barber.

   → Instead _____ his own hair, Jake should go to a barber.

8. Mr. and Mrs. Reed have always saved for a rainy day. They believe _____ that.

   → Mr. and Mrs. Reed believe _____ _____ for a rainy day.

9. I may fall on my face and make a fool of myself. I'm worried _____ that.

   → I'm worried _____ on my face and

_____

*If necessary, refer to Appendix 1 for a list of preposition combinations.

_____ a fool of myself when I walk up the steps to receive my diploma.

10. The children are going to go to Disneyland. They're excited _____ that.

→ The children are excited _____ to Disneyland.

11. Their parents are going to Disneyland, too. They are looking forward _____ that.

→ Their parents are looking forward _____ there, too.

10-8 USING *BY* AND *WITH* TO EXPRESS HOW SOMETHING IS DONE

(a) Pat turned off the tape recorder **by pushing** the stop button.	***By*** + *a gerund* is used to express how something is done.
(b) Mary goes to work **by bus**. (c) Andrea stirred her coffee **with a spoon**.	***By*** or ***with*** followed by a noun is also used to express how something is done.

BY IS USED FOR MEANS OF TRANSPORTATION AND COMMUNICATION:

by (air)plane	*by subway**	*by mail	*by air
*by boat	*by taxi	*by (tele)phone	*by land
*by bus	*by train	*by fax	*by sea
*by car	*by foot* (OR *on foot*)		

OTHERS:
by chance
by choice
by mistake
by check (but *in cash*)
by hand***

WITH IS USED FOR INSTRUMENTS OR PARTS OF THE BODY:
I cut down the tree *with an ax* (by using an ax).
I swept the floor *with a broom*.
She pointed to a spot on the map *with her finger*.

*airplane = American English   *aeroplane* = British English
**by subway = American English   *by underground, by tube* = British English
***The expression **by hand** is usually used to mean that something was made by a person, not by a machine: *This rug was made **by hand**.* (A person, not a machine, made this rug.) COMPARE: *I touched his shoulder **with my hand**.*

☐ **EXERCISE 14:** Complete the following by using *by* + a GERUND. Use the words in the
list or your own words.

eat	smile	watch
drink	wag	wave
guess	wash	✔write
grow		

1. Students practice written English _____ ***by writing*** _____ compositions.

2. We clean our clothes _____ them in soap and water.

3. I save money on food _____ my own vegetables.

4. Khalid improved his English _____ a lot of TV.

5. We show other people we are happy _____.

6. We satisfy our hunger _____ something.

7. We quench our thirst _____ something.

8. I figured out what "quench" means _____.

9. Alex caught my attention _____ his arms in the air.

10. My dog shows me she is happy _____ her tail.

Complete the following with your own words. Use **by** *and* GERUNDS.

11. Students show teachers they want to say something _____
_____ their hands.

12. You can destroy bacteria in meat _____ it.

13. You can cook an egg _____ it, _____ it,
or _____ it.

14. After work, I relax _____ or _____.

15. Each of you, in your own small way, can help conserve the world's
natural resources _____.

☐ **EXERCISE 15:** Complete the sentences with *by* or *with*.

1. I opened the door _____ ***with*** _____ a key.

2. I went to Cherryville _____ ***by*** _____ bus.

3. I dried the dishes _____ a dishtowel.

4. I went from Portland to San Francisco
_____ train.

5. Paul dug a hole _____ a shovel.

6. Ted drew a straight line _____ a ruler.

7. Is there any way you could touch the ceiling _____ your foot?

8. Some advertisers try to reach target audiences _____ mail.

9. Rebecca tightened the screw in the corner of her eyeglasses _____ her fingernail.

10. I called Bill "Paul" _____ mistake.

11. The fastest way to send a copy of a piece of paper halfway around the world is _____ fax.

12. The chef sliced the partially frozen meat into thin strips _____ a razor-sharp knife.

10-9 USING GERUNDS AS SUBJECTS; USING *IT* + INFINITIVE

(a) **Riding** horses is fun. (b) **It** is fun **to ride** horses.	(a) and (b) have the same meaning. In (a): A gerund (*riding*) is the subject of the sentence.* Notice: The verb (*is*) is singular because a gerund is singular.
(c) **Coming** to class on time is important. (d) **It** is important **to come** to class on time.	In (b): The word **it** is used as the subject of the sentence. The word **it** has the same meaning as the infinitive phrase at the end of the sentence: **it** means *to ride horses*.

*It is also correct (but less common) to use an infinitive as the subject of a sentence: *To ride horses is fun.*

☐ **EXERCISE 16—ORAL:** Make sentences with the same meaning by using *it* + INFINITIVE.

1. Having good friends is important. → *It is important to have good friends.*
2. Playing tennis is fun.
3. Being polite to other people is important.
4. Learning about other cultures is interesting.
5. Walking alone at night in that part of the city is dangerous.
6. Is learning a second language difficult?
7. Is riding a motorcycle easy?
8. Having a cold isn't much fun.
9. Learning a second language takes a long time.
10. Cooking a soft-boiled egg takes three minutes.

□ **EXERCISE 17—ORAL:** Make sentences with the same meaning by using a GERUND as the subject.

1. It is important to get daily exercise.
   → *Getting daily exercise is important.*
2. It is fun to meet new people.
3. It is easy to cook rice.
4. It is boring to spend the whole weekend in the dorm.
5. It is relaxing to take a long walk.
6. Is it difficult to learn a second language?
7. It isn't hard to make friends.
8. It is wrong to cheat during a test.
9. Is it dangerous to smoke cigarettes?
10. Is it expensive to live in an apartment?
11. It isn't easy to live in a foreign country.
12. It takes time to make new friends.

□ **EXERCISE 18—ORAL:** Answer the questions.

STUDENT A: Use *it* + *infinitives*.
STUDENT B: Use *gerunds*.

1. Which is easier: to make money or to spend money?
   → A: *It is easier to spend money than (it is) to make money.*
   → B: *Spending money is easier than making money.*
2. Which is more fun: to study at the library or to go to a movie?
3. Which is more difficult: to write English or to read English?
4. Which is easier: to write English or to speak English?
5. Which is more expensive: to go to a movie or to go to a concert?
6. Which is more interesting: to talk to people or to watch people?
7. Which is more comfortable: to wear shoes or to go barefoot?
8. Which is more satisfying: to give gifts or to receive them?
9. Which is more dangerous: to ride in a car or to ride in an airplane?
10. Which is more important: to come to class on time or to get an extra hour of sleep in the morning?
11. Which is better: to light one candle or to curse the darkness?

10-10 *IT* + INFINITIVE: USING *FOR (SOMEONE)*

(a) *You* should study hard. (b) It is important *for you* to study hard. (c) *Mary* should study hard. (d) It is important *for Mary* to study hard. (e) *We* don't have to go to the meeting. (f) It isn't necessary *for us* to go to the meeting. (g) *A dog* can't talk. (h) It is impossible *for a dog* to talk.	(a) and (b) have a similar meaning. Notice the pattern in (b): *it is* + *adjective* + *for* (*someone*) + *infinitive phrase*

☐ **EXERCISE 19:** Use the given information to complete each sentence. Use *for* (*someone*) and an INFINITIVE PHRASE in each completion.

1. *Students should do their homework.*

   It's important _____ **for students to do their homework.** _____

2. *Teachers should speak clearly.*

   It's important _____

3. *We don't have to hurry.*

   There's plenty of time. It isn't necessary _____

4. *A fish can't live out of water for more than a few minutes.*

   It's impossible _____

5. *Students have to budget their time carefully.*

   It's necessary _____

6. *A child usually can't sit still for a long time.*

   It's difficult _____

7. *My family always eats turkey on Thanksgiving Day.*

   It's traditional _____

8. *People can take vacation trips to the moon.*

   Will it be possible _____ within the next fifty years?

9. *I usually can't understand Mr. Allen.*

   It's hard _____ He talks too fast.

10. *I can understand our teacher.*

    It's easy _____

11. *The guests usually wait until the hostess begins to eat.*

    At a formal dinner party, it's customary _____

    After she takes the first bite, the guests also start to eat.

12. *The bride usually feeds the groom the first piece of wedding cake.*

    It's traditional _____

10-11 INFINITIVE OF PURPOSE: USING *IN ORDER TO*

Why did you go to the post office? (a) I went to the post office *because I wanted to mail a letter*. (b) I went to the post office *in order to mail a letter*. (c) I went to the post office *to mail a letter*.	***In order to*** expresses purpose. ***In order to*** answers the question "Why?"
	In (c): ***in order*** is frequently omitted. (a), (b) and (c) have the same meaning.
(d) I went to the post office *for some stamps*. (e) I went to the post office *to buy some stamps*. (f) INCORRECT: I went to the post office for to buy some stamps. (g) INCORRECT: I went to the post office for buying some stamps.	***For*** is also used to express purpose, but it is a preposition and is followed by a noun phrase, as in (d).

□ **EXERCISE 20:** Add *in order* to the sentences whenever possible.

1. I went to the bank to cash a check.

   → *I went to the bank in order to cash a check.*

2. I'd like to see that movie.

   → (*No change. The infinitive does not express purpose.*)

3. Sam went to the hospital to visit a friend.

4. I need to go to the bank today.

5. I need to go to the bank today to deposit my pay check.

6. On my way home from school, I stopped at the drugstore to buy some shampoo.

7. Carmen looked in her dictionary to find the correct spelling of a word.

8. Masako went to the cafeteria to eat lunch.

9. Jack and Linda have decided to get married.

10. Pedro watches TV to improve his English.

11. I didn't forget to pay my rent.

12. Kim wrote to the university to ask for a catalog.

13. Sally touched my shoulder to get my attention.

14. Donna expects to graduate next spring.

15. Jerry needs to go to the bookstore to buy a spiral notebook.

□ **EXERCISE 21:** Complete the sentences by using *to* or *for*.

1. I went to Chicago ___*for*___ a visit.

2. I went to Chicago ___*to*___ visit my aunt and uncle.

3. I take long walks _____ relax.

4. I take long walks _____ relaxation.

5. I'm going to school _____ a good education.

6. I'm going to school _____ get a good education.

7. I'm not going to school just _____ have fun.

8. I'm not going to school just _____ fun.

9. I went to the store _____ some bread and milk.

10. I went to the store _____ get some bread and milk.

11. I turned on the radio _____ listen to the news.

12. I listened to the radio _____ news about the earthquake in Peru.

13. We wear coats in the winter _____ keep warm.

14. We wear coats in the winter _____ warmth.

☐ **EXERCISE 22—ORAL (BOOKS CLOSED):** Answer "why-questions" in your own words. Show purpose by using an infinitive phrase or a "*for*-phrase."

    Example: Yesterday you turned on the TV. Why?

    Response: Yesterday I turned on the TV (to listen to the news, for the latest news about the earthquake, etc.).

1. You went to the supermarket. Why?
2. You need to go to the bookstore.
3. You went to the post office.
4. You have to go to the library.
5. You went to the health clinic.
6. You reached into your pocket/purse.
7. You came to this school.
8. You borrowed some money from (. . .).
9. You stopped at the service station.
10. You play (*soccer, tennis, etc.*).
11. You had to go out last night.
12. You're going to go to (*Chicago*).

☐ **EXERCISE 23—ORAL:** Combine the given ideas to make sentences using infinitives of purpose. Begin each of your sentences with "*Yesterday I. . . .*"

    Example: go shopping/go downtown

    Response: *Yesterday I went downtown (in order) to go shopping.*

1. call the dentist's office/make an appointment
   → *Yesterday I . . . .*
2. study for a test/go to the library
3. get rid of my headache/take an aspirin
4. go to the laundromat/wash my clothes
5. have to run/get to class on time
6. go to (*name of a place*)/eat lunch
7. make a reservation to go to . . . /call the travel agency
8. ask the teacher a question/stay after class
9. write a letter to my parents/ask them for some money
10. listen to a baseball game/turn on the radio

11. get a cup of coffee between classes/borrow some money from (. . .)

12. stand in the doorway of a store/get out of the rain while I was waiting for the bus

10-12   USING INFINITIVES WITH *TOO* AND *ENOUGH*

TOO + ADJECTIVE + (FOR SOMEONE) + INFINITIVE (a) A piano is **too** *heavy* *to lift*. (b) That box is **too** *heavy* ***for me*** *to lift*. (c) That box is **too** *heavy* ***for Bob*** *to lift*.	Infinitives often follow expressions with **too**. **Too** comes in front of an adjective. In the speaker's mind, the use of **too** implies a negative result. COMPARE: *The box is too heavy. I can't lift it.* *The box is very heavy, but I can lift it.*
ENOUGH + NOUN + INFINITIVE (d) I don't have **enough** *money* *to buy* that car. (e) Did you have **enough** *time* *to finish* the test?	
ADJECTIVE + ENOUGH + INFINITIVE (f) Jimmy isn't *old* **enough** *to go* to school. (g) Are you *hungry* **enough** *to eat* three sandwiches?	Infinitives often follow expressions with **enough**. **Enough** comes in front of a noun.★ **Enough** follows an adjective.

★*Enough* can also follow a noun: *I don't have **money enough** to buy that car.* In everyday English, however, **enough** usually comes in front of a noun.

☐ **EXERCISE 24:** Make sentences by putting the following in the correct order.

1. time/to go to the park tomorrow/I don't have/enough

   I don't have enough time to go to the park tomorrow.

2. to touch the ceiling/too/I'm/short

   _____

3. to pay his bills/money/Tom doesn't have/enough

_____

4. for me/this tea is/hot/to drink/too

_____

5. to eat breakfast this morning/time/I didn't have/enough

_____

6. enough/to stay home alone/old/Susie isn't

_____

7. too/to stay home alone/young/Susie is

_____

8. late/to go to the movie/for us/too/it's

_____

□ **EXERCISE 25—ORAL:** Combine the sentences. Use *too*.

    1. We can't go swimming today. It's very cold.
      → *It's too cold (for us) to go swimming today.*
    2. I couldn't finish my homework last night. I was very sleepy.
    3. This jacket is very small. I can't wear it.
    4. Mike couldn't go to his aunt's housewarming party. He was very busy.
    5. I live far from school. I can't walk there.
    6. Some movies are very violent. Children shouldn't watch them.

Combine the sentences. Use **enough.**

    7. I can't reach the top shelf. I'm not that tall.
      → *I'm not tall enough to reach the top shelf.*
    8. I can't lift a horse. I'm not that strong.
    9. It's not warm today. We can't go outside in shorts and sandals.
   10. I didn't stay home and miss work. I wasn't really sick, but I didn't feel good all day.

□ **EXERCISE 26:** Complete the following sentences. Use INFINITIVES in the completions.

    1. The weather is too cold _____

    2. Timmy is two years old. He's too young _____

    3. Timmy isn't old enough _____

    4. That suitcase is too heavy _____

5. Ann isn't strong enough _____

6. Last night I was too tired _____

7. Yesterday I was too busy _____

8. A Mercedes-Benz is too expensive _____

9. I don't have enough money _____

10. Yesterday I didn't have enough time _____

11. A teenager is old enough _____

12. This coffee is too hot _____

13. I know enough English _____

14. The test was too long _____

15. I'm too short _____

16. I'm not tall enough _____

☐ **EXERCISE 27—ERROR ANALYSIS:** All of the following sentences contain mistakes. Find and correct the mistakes.

1. Do you enjoy to go to the zoo?
   (*Correction: Do you enjoy going to the zoo?*)

2. I went to the store for getting some toothpaste.

3. Did you go to shopping yesterday?

4. I usually go to the cafeteria for to get a cup of coffee in the morning.

5. Bob needed to went downtown yesterday.

6. I cut the rope by a knife.

7. I thanked him for drive me to the airport.

8. Is difficult to learn a second language.

9. It is important getting an education.

10. Timmy isn't enough old to get married.

11. Do you want go to swimming tomorrow?

12. I went to the bank for cashing a check.

13. I was to sleepy to finish my homework last night.

14. Is easy this exercise to do.

15. Last night too tired no do my homework.

16. I've never gone to sailing, but I would like.

☐ EXERCISE 28—ORAL: Form small groups. Make a list of several topics that can be used for a one-minute impromptu speech. The topics should be GERUND PHRASES. Exchange topics with another group. After your group has its topics, each member in turn should give a one-minute speech to the rest of the group. One group member should keep time. After all the speeches have been given, choose one speech from your group to be presented to the rest of the class.

Examples of topics: eating at fast-food restaurants, traveling to a foreign country, taking care of your health.

☐ EXERCISE 29—WRITTEN: What do you do for fun and recreation in your spare time? Write about one or two spare-time activities that you enjoy. What do you do? Where? When? Why? Mention some interesting experiences. Try to get your readers interested in doing the same things in their free time. Do you enjoy exploring caves? Is playing tennis one of your passions? Have you ever gone skydiving? Maybe collecting ceramic horses is one of your hobbies. Have you ever gone waterskiing? Do you enjoy simple pleasures such as walking in a park? Do you go jogging for recreation? Maybe watching sports on television is your way of relaxing. It is important for all of us to have spare-time activities that we enjoy. What are yours?

10-13 MORE PHRASAL VERBS (SEPARABLE)★

ask out	*ask someone to go on a date*
call back	*return a telephone call*
call off	*cancel*
call up	*make a telephone call*
give back	*return something to someone*
hang up	*(1) hang on a hanger or a hook; (2) end a telephone call*
pay back	*return money to someone*
put away	*put something in its usual or proper place*
put back	*return something to its original place*
put out	*extinguish (stop) a fire, a cigarette, a cigar*
shut off	*stop a machine or light, turn off*
try on	*put on clothing to see if it fits*
turn down	*decrease the volume*
turn up	*increase the volume*

★See 9-8 and 9-9 for more information about phrasal verbs.

□ **EXERCISE 30:** Complete the sentences with pronouns and particles.

1. A: Could you lend me a couple of bucks?

   B: Sure.

   A: Thanks. I'll pay _____*you back*_____ tomorrow.

2. A: The radio is too loud. Could you please turn _____?

   B: Sure.

3. A: I can't hear the TV. Could you please turn _____?

   B: I'd be glad to.

4. A: Have you heard from Jack lately?

   B: Yes. He called _____ last night.*

5. A: Someone's at the door. Can I call _____ in a few
   minutes?

   B: Sure.

6. A: Where's my coat?

   B: I hung _____.

7. A: Is the oven on?

   B: No. I shut _____.

---

*There is no difference in meaning between *He called me last night* and *He called me up last night.*

8. A: May I borrow your small calculator tonight?

   B: Sure.

   A: I'll give _____ to you tomorrow.

   B: Okay.

9. A: You can't smoke that cigarette in the auditorium. You'd better put

   _____ before we go in.

   B: Okay.

10. A: Do you have any plans for Saturday night?

    B: Yes. I have a date. Jim Olsen asked _____.

11. A: Did you take my eraser off of my desk?

    B: Yes, but I put _____ on your desk when I was

    finished.

    A: Oh? It's not here.

    B: Look under your notebook.

    A: Ah. There it is. Thanks.

12. A: Your toys are all over the floor, kids. Before you go to bed, be sure to

    put _____.

    B: Okay, Daddy.

13. A: Did you go to Kathy's party last night?

    B: She didn't have a party. She called _____.

14. A: This is a nice-looking coat. Why don't you try _____?

    B: How much does it cost?

CHAPTER 11
Passive Sentences

11-1 ACTIVE SENTENCES AND PASSIVE SENTENCES

(a) ACTIVE: Bob *mailed* the package. (b) PASSIVE: The package *was mailed* by Bob.	(a) and (b) have the same meaning.
(c) S V O Bob | mailed | the package. S V "by-phrase" The package | was mailed | by Bob.	In (c): The **object** of an active sentence becomes the **subject** of a passive sentence.
(d) S V O Bob | mailed | the package. S V "by-phrase" The package | was mailed | by Bob.	In (d): The **subject** of an active sentence is the **object** of *by* in the "*by*-phrase" in a passive sentence.
(e) ACTIVE: The teacher *corrects* our homework. (f) PASSIVE: Our homework *is corrected* by the teacher. (g) ACTIVE: Mr. Lee *will teach* this class. (h) PASSIVE: This class *will be taught* by Mr. Lee.	Form of all passive verbs: **BE + PAST PARTICIPLE.** **BE** can be in any of its forms: *am, is, are, was, were, has been, have been, will be,* etc. **THE PAST PARTICIPLE** follows **BE**. For regular verbs, the past participle ends in *-ed* (e.g., *mailed, corrected*). Some past participles are irregular (e.g., *taught*). See Chart 2-4.

11-2 TENSE FORMS OF PASSIVE VERBS

Notice that all the passive verbs are formed with **BE** + **PAST PARTICIPLE**.				
TENSE	ACTIVE		PASSIVE	
SIMPLE PRESENT	The news The news The news	*surprises* me. *surprises* Sam. *surprises* us.	I Sam We	*am surprised* by the news. *is surprised* by the news. *are surprised* by the news.
SIMPLE PAST	The news The news	*surprised* me. *surprised* us.	I We	*was surprised* by the news. *were surprised* by the news.
PRESENT PERFECT	Bob Bob	*has mailed* the letter. *has mailed* the letters.	The letter The letters	*has been mailed* by Bob. *have been mailed* by Bob.
FUTURE	Bob Bob *is going to mail* the letter.	*will mail* the letter.	The letter The letter *is going to be mailed* by Bob.	*will be mailed* by Bob.

☐ **EXERCISE 1:** Change the active verbs to passive verbs. Write the subject of the passive sentence.

1. SIMPLE PRESENT

   a. The teacher *helps* **me**.   _____**I**_____ _____**am helped**_____ by the teacher.

   b. The teacher *helps* **Jane**.   _____ _____ by the teacher.

   c. The teacher *helps* **us**.   _____ _____ by the teacher.

2. SIMPLE PAST

   a. The teacher *helped* **me**.   _____ _____ by the teacher.

   b. The teacher *helped* **them**.   _____ _____ by the teacher.

3. PRESENT PERFECT

   a. The teacher *has helped* **Joe**.   _____ _____ by the teacher.

   b. The teacher *has helped* **us**.   _____ _____ by the teacher.

4. FUTURE

   a. The teacher *will help* **me**.   _____ _____ by the teacher.

   b. The teacher *is going to help* **me**.   _____ _____ by the teacher.

   c. The teacher *will help* **Tim**.   _____ _____ by the teacher.

   d. The teacher *is going to help* **Tim**.   _____ _____ by the teacher.

□ **EXERCISE 2:** Change the verbs to the passive. Do not change the tense.

		BE +	PAST PARTICIPLE	
1. Bob *mailed* the package.	The package	**was**	**mailed**	by Bob.
2. Mr. Catt *delivers* our mail.	Our mail	_____	_____	by Mr. Catt.
3. The children *have eaten* the cake.	The cake	_____	_____	by the children.
4. Linda *wrote* that letter.	That letter	_____	_____	by Linda.
5. The jeweler *is going to fix* my watch.	My watch	_____	_____	by the jeweler.
6. Ms. Bond *will teach* our class.	Our class	_____	_____	by Ms. Bond.
7. That company *employs* many people.	Many people	_____	_____	by that company.
8. That company *has hired* Sue.	Sue	_____	_____	by that company.
9. The secretary *is going to fax* the letters.	The letters	_____	_____	by the secretary.
10. A college student *bought* my old car.	My old car	_____	_____	by a college student.
11. Mr. Adams *will do* the work.	The work	_____	_____	by Mr. Adams.
12. Mr. Fox *washed* the windows.	The windows	_____	_____	by Mr. Fox.

□ **EXERCISE 3:** Change the sentences from active to passive.

1. Ms. Hopkins invited me to dinner.

_____ *I was invited to dinner by Ms. Hopkins.* _____

2. Thomas Edison invented the phonograph.

_____

3. Water surrounds an island.

_____

4. A maid will clean our hotel room.

_____

5. A plumber is going to fix the leaky faucet.

_____

6. A doctor has examined the sick child.

_____

7. The police arrested James Swan.

_____

8. A large number of people speak Spanish.

_____

9. The secretary is going to answer the letter.

_____

10. The teacher's explanation confused Carlos.

_____

_____

11. My mistake embarrassed me.

_____

_____

12. Helicopters fascinate children.

_____

_____

13. Shakespeare wrote *Hamlet*.*

_____

14. This news will amaze you.

_____

_____

*Notice that *Hamlet*, the title of a play, is printed in italics. In handwritten or typed sentences, the title of a book or a play is underlined.

    Printed: Tolstoy wrote *War and Peace*.

    Handwritten: *Tolstoy wrote War and Peace.*

    Typed: Tolstoy wrote <u>War and Peace</u>.

☐ **EXERCISE 4:** Change the active sentences to passive sentences that have the same meaning and tense.

ACTIVE   PASSIVE

1. a. The news surprised John.   _**John was surprised**_ ___ by the news.

    b. The news didn't surprise me.   _**I wasn't surprised**_ ___ by the news.

    c. Did the news surprise you?   _**Were you surprised**_ ___ by the news?

2. a. The news surprises Erin. _____ by the news.

    b. The news doesn't surprise us. _____ by the news.

    c. Does the news surprise you? _____ by the news?

3. a. The news will shock Steve. _____ by the news.

    b. The news won't shock Jean. _____ by the news.

    c. Will the news shock Pat? _____ by the news?

4. a. Liz wrote that petition. _____ by Liz.

    b. Don didn't write it. _____ by Don.

    c. Did Ryan write it? _____ by Ryan?

PETITION

     We, the undersigned, believe that the house at 3205 Tree Street is an historic building. We believe that it should not be destroyed in order to build a fast-food restaurant at that location.

Robert E. Miller   *Wm. H. Brock*

Elizabeth J. Wilson   *Ms. Catherine Ann Jackson*

James Walsh   *An Binh Nguyen*

Alicia Alvarez

---

5. a. Bob has signed the petition. _____ by Bob.

    b. Paul hasn't signed it. _____ by Paul.

    c. Has Jim signed it yet? _____ by Jim yet?

6. a. Sue is going to sign it. _____ by Sue.

    b. John isn't going to sign it. _____ by John.

    c. Is Carol going to sign it? _____ by Carol?

☐ **EXERCISE 5:** Change the sentences from active to passive.

1. A thief stole Ann's purse.

   **Ann's purse was stolen by a thief.**

2. Did a cat kill the bird?

   _____

3. My cat didn't kill the bird.

   _____

4. A squirrel didn't bite the jogger.

   _____

5. A dog bit the jogger.

   _____

6. Do a large number of people speak English?

   _____

7. Did Johnny break the window?

   _____

8. Is the janitor going to fix the window?

   _____

9. More than one hundred people have signed the petition.

   _____

10. Did Shakespeare write *A Midsummer Night's Dream?*

_____

11. Ernest Hemingway didn't write *A Midsummer Night's Dream.*

_____

12. Will a maid clean our hotel room?

_____

13. Does the hotel provide clean towels?

_____

14. Sometimes my inability to understand spoken English frustrates me.

_____

11-3 TRANSITIVE AND INTRANSITIVE VERBS

(a) **TRANSITIVE VERBS**
ACTIVE: Bob *mailed* the letter.
PASSIVE: The letter *was mailed* by Bob.
 	
(b) **INTRANSITIVE VERBS**
ACTIVE: An accident *happened.*
PASSIVE: *(not possible)*
 	
(c) INCORRECT: An accident was happened.
	Only transitive verbs can be used in the passive.
	A transitive verb is a verb that is followed by an object. Examples:
	   S **V** **O**
	  Bob mailed the letter.
	  Mr. Lee signed the check.
	  A cat killed the bird.

	An intransitive verb is a verb that is not followed by an object. Example:
	   S **V**
	  An accident happened.
	    John came to our house.
	    I slept well last night.
	
	An intransitive verb CANNOT be used in the passive.

☐ **EXERCISE 6:** Change the sentences to the passive if possible. Write the symbol "Ø" if a sentence cannot be changed to the passive.

1. Jack walked to school yesterday. _____Ø_____

2. We stayed in a hotel. _____

3. Susie broke the window. _____

4. The leaves fell to the ground. _____

5. I slept at my friend's house last night. _____

6. The second baseman caught the ball. _____

7. Ann's cat died last week. _____

8. That book belongs to me. _____

9. The airplane arrived twenty minutes late. _____

10. The teacher announced a quiz. _____

11. I agree with George. _____

12. Do you agree with me? _____

13. Dick went to the doctor's office. _____

14. An accident happened at the corner of Third and Main. _____

15. An accident occurred at the corner of Third and Main. _____

16. Many people saw the accident. _____

11-4 USING THE "*BY*-PHRASE"

(a) This sweater *was made* **by my aunt**.	The "*by*-phrase" is used in passive sentences when it is important to know who performs an action. In (a): *by my aunt* is important information.
(b) That sweater *was made* in Korea. (*by someone*) (c) Spanish *is spoken* in Colombia. (*by people*) (d) That house *was built* in 1940. (*by someone*) (e) Rice *is grown* in many countries. (*by people*)	Uusually there is no "*by*-phrase" in a passive sentence. The passive is used when it is not known or not important to know exactly who performs an action. In (b): The exact person (or people) who made the sweater is not known and is not important to know, so there is no "*by*-phrase" in the passive sentence.

☐ **EXERCISE 7:** Change the sentence from active to passive. Include the "*by*-phrase" only if necessary.

1. Bob Smith built that house.

    That house was built by Bob Smith. _____

2. Someone built this house in 1904.

    This house was built in 1904.   (*by someone = unnecessary*)

3. People grow rice in India.

    _____

4. People speak Spanish in Venezuela.

    _____

5. Do people speak Spanish in Peru?

_____

6. Alexander Graham Bell invented the telephone.

_____

7. When did someone invent the wheel?

_____

8. People sell hammers at a hardware store.

_____

9. People use hammers to pound nails.

_____

10. The president has canceled the meeting.

_____

11. Someone has canceled the soccer game.

_____

12. Someone will list my name in the new telephone directory.

_____

13. Charles Darwin wrote _The Origin of Species._

_____

14. Someone published _The Origin of Species_ in 1859.

_____

15. Someone serves beer and wine at that restaurant.

_____

"DEEP ASLEEP... DEEP ASLEEP..
YOU FEEL VERY SLEEPY..., DEEP..."

16. Has anyone ever hypnotized you?

_____

17. Something confused me in class yesterday.

_____

18. Something embarrassed me yesterday.

_____

19. Someone has changed the name of this street from Bay Avenue to Martin Luther King Way.

_____

20. Someone filmed many of the Tarzan movies in the rain forest in Puerto Rico.

_____

_____

_____

"CAMERA! ACTION!"

□ **EXERCISE 8—ORAL:** Change the sentences from active to passive. Include the "*by*-phrase" only if it contains important information.

    Example: Someone has invited us to a party.
    Response: We have been invited to a party.

    Example: No one has invited John to the party.
    Response: John hasn't been invited to the party.

1. Someone established the Red Cross in 1864.
2. When did someone establish this school?
3. Someone collects the garbage on Thursdays.

4. No one will collect the garbage tomorrow.
5. People spell "writing" with one "t."
6. People don't spell "writing" with two "t's."
7. People spell "written" with two "t's."
8. Someone is going to build a new hospital next year.
9. When did someone build the Suez Canal?
10. Olga wrote that composition.
11. The University of Minnesota has accepted me.
12. People don't teach calculus in elementary school.
13. People held the 1988 Summer Olympics in Seoul, Korea.
14. No one delivers the mail on holidays.
15. Will someone deliver the mail tomorrow?
16. Someone made my tape recorder in Japan.
17. Where did someone make your tape recorder?
18. My grandfather made that table.
19. No one has ever hypnotized me.
20. Did my directions confuse you?

☐ **EXERCISE 9:** Complete the sentences with the correct form of the verb (active or passive) in parentheses.

1. Yesterday our teacher (*arrive*) _____ *arrived* _____ five minutes late.

2. The morning paper (*read*) _____ by over 200,000 people every day.

3. Last night my favorite TV program (*interrupt*) _____ _____ by a special news bulletin.

4. That's not my coat. It (*belong*) _____ to Louise.

5. Our mail (*deliver*) _____ before noon every day.

6. The "b" in "comb" (*pronounce, not*) _____. It is silent.

7. A bad accident (*happen*) _____ on Highway 95 last night.

8. When I (*arrive*) _____ at the airport yesterday, I (*meet*) _____ by my cousin and a couple of her friends.

9. Yesterday I (*hear*) _____ about Margaret's divorce. I (*surprise*) _____ by the news. Janice (*shock*) _____.

10. A new house (*build*) _____ next to ours next year.

11. Roberto (*write*) _____ this composition last week. That one (*write*) _____ by Abdullah.

12. Radium (*discover*) _____ by Marie and Pierre Curie in 1898.

13. At the soccer game yesterday, the winning goal (*kick*) _____ by Luigi. Over 100,000 people (*attend*) _____ the soccer game.

14. A: Do you understand the explanation in the book?

    B: No, I don't. I (*confuse*) _____ by it.

15. A: Where are you going to go to school next year?

    B: I (*accept*) _____ by Shoreline Community College.

16. A: I think football is too violent.

    B: I (*agree*) _____ with you. I (*prefer*) _____ baseball.

17. A: When (*your bike, steal*) _____?

    B: Two days ago.

18. A: (*you, pay*) _____ your electric bill yet?

    B: No, I haven't, but I'd better pay it today. If I don't, my electricity (*shut off*) _____ by the power company.

19. A: Did you hear about the accident?

    B: No. What (*happen*) _____?

    A: A bicyclist (*hit*) _____ by a taxi in front of the dorm.

    B: (*the bicyclist, injure*) _____?

    A: Yes. Someone (*call*) _____ an ambulance. The bicyclist (*take*) _____ to City Hospital and (*treat*) _____ in the emergency ward for cuts and bruises.

    B: What (*happen*) _____ to the taxi driver?

    A: He (*arrest*) _____ for reckless driving.

    B: He's lucky that the bicyclist (*kill, not*) _____.

20. The Eiffel Tower (*be*) _____ in Paris, France. It (*visit*) _____ by millions of people every year. It (*design*) _____ by Alexandre Eiffel (1832–1923). It (*erect*) _____ in 1889 for the Paris exposition. Since that time, it (*be*) _____ the most famous landmark in Paris. Today it (*recognize*) _____ by people throughout the world.

11-5 THE PASSIVE FORMS OF THE PRESENT AND PAST PROGRESSIVE

ACTIVE	PASSIVE	
The secretary *is copying* some letters. Someone *is building* a new hospital.	(a) Some letters **are being copied** by the secretary. (b) A new hospital **is being built**.	Passive form of the present progressive: am is are + **being** + PAST PARTICIPLE
The secretary *was copying* some letters. Someone *was building* a new hospital.	(c) Some letters **were being copied** by the secretary. (d) A new hospital **was being built**.	Passive form of the past progressive: was were + **being** + PAST PARTICIPLE

☐ **EXERCISE 10:** Change the sentences from active to passive. Include the ''*by*-phrase'' only if it contains important information.

1. Someone is building a new house on Elm Street.

_____

2. The Smith Construction Company is building that house.

_____

3. Yoko is reading this sentence.

_____

4. We can't use our classroom today because someone is painting it.

We can't use our classroom today because _____

5. We couldn't use our classroom yesterday because someone was painting it.

We couldn't use our classroom yesterday because _____

6. We can't use the language lab today because someone is fixing the equipment.

We can't use the language lab today because _____

7. We couldn't use the language lab yesterday because someone was fixing the equipment.

We couldn't use the language lab yesterday because _____

8. Someone is repairing my shoes.

_____

9. Someone was repairing my shoes.

_____

10. Someone is organizing a student trip to the art museum.

_____

11-6 PASSIVE MODAL AUXILIARIES

ACTIVE MODAL AUXILIARIES	PASSIVE MODAL AUXILIARIES (MODAL + BE + PAST PARTICIPLE)	Modal auxiliaries are often used in the passive.
Bob *will mail* it. Bob *can mail* it. Bob *should mail* it. Bob *ought to mail* it. Bob *must mail* it. Bob *has to mail* it. Bob *may mail* it. Bob *might mail* it.	It *will be mailed* by Bob. It *can be mailed* by Bob. It *should be mailed* by Bob. It *ought to be mailed* by Bob. It *must be mailed* by Bob. It *has to be mailed* by Bob. It *may be mailed* by Bob. It *might be mailed* by Bob.	FORM: modal + **BE** + past participle See Chapter 5 for information about the meanings and uses of modal auxiliaries.

☐ **EXERCISE 11:** Change the sentences from active to passive. Include the "*by*-phrase" only if it contains important information.

1. Someone might cancel class. _____ ***Class might be canceled.*** _____

2. A doctor can prescribe medicine. _____

3. People should plant tomatoes in the spring. _____

4. Mr. Hook must sign this report. _____

5. Someone may build a new post office on First Street.

_____

6. People may not sell beer to minors. _____

7. People can reach me at 555–3815. _____

8. People have to place stamps in the upper right-hand corner of an

envelope.

_____

9. Someone ought to paint that fence. _____

10. People cannot control the weather. _____

11. Someone had to fix our car before we left for Chicago.

_____

12. All of the students must do the assignment.

_____

11-7 SUMMARY: PASSIVE VERB FORMS

REMINDER: All passive verbs are formed with **BE** + **PAST PARTICIPLE**.

ACTIVE			PASSIVE		
Dr. Gray	*helps*	Tom.	Tom	*is helped*	by Dr. Gray.
Dr. Gray	*is helping*	Tom.	Tom	*is being helped*	by Dr. Gray.
Dr. Gray	*has helped*	Tom.	Tom	*has been helped*	by Dr. Gray.
Dr. Gray	*helped*	Tom.	Tom	*was helped*	by Dr. Gray.
Dr. Gray	*was helping*	Tom.	Tom	*was being helped*	by Dr. Gray.
Dr. Gray	*had helped*	Tom.	Tom	*had been helped*	by Dr. Gray.
Dr. Gray	*is going to help*	Tom.	Tom	*is going to be helped*	by Dr. Gray.
Dr. Gray	*will help*	Tom.	Tom	*will be helped*	by Dr. Gray.
Dr. Gray	*can help*	Tom.	Tom	*can be helped*	by Dr. Gray.
Dr. Gray	*should help*	Tom.	Tom	*should be helped*	by Dr. Gray.
Dr. Gray	*ought to help*	Tom.	Tom	*ought to be helped*	by Dr. Gray.
Dr. Gray	*must help*	Tom.	Tom	*must be helped*	by Dr. Gray.
Dr. Gray	*has to help*	Tom.	Tom	*has to be helped*	by Dr. Gray.
Dr. Gray	*may help*	Tom.	Tom	*may be helped*	by Dr. Gray.
Dr. Gray	*might help*	Tom.	Tom	*might be helped*	by Dr. Gray.

□ **EXERCISE 12—ORAL (BOOKS CLOSED):** Practice using passive forms.

Example: Someone will paint this room.
Response: This room will be painted.

I. *Someone . . . this room.*
1. should paint
2. ought to paint
3. must paint
4. will paint
5. is going to paint
6. may paint
7. is painting
8. was painting
9. has painted
10. painted

II. *Someone . . .*
11. must solve this problem.
12. is preparing dinner.
13. has to pay this bill.
14. should eat this food.
15. will mail the package.
16. may raise the price of gas.
17. has made a mistake.
18. ought to wash the windows.

III.
19. No one has washed the dishes yet.
20. Someone should wash them soon.
21. No one has sent that package yet.
22. Someone should send it soon.
23. No one has solved that problem yet.
24. Someone must solve it soon.
25. No one invited me to the party.
26. Did someone invite you to the party?
27. Someone built the Suez Canal in the nineteenth century.
28. No one built the Suez Canal in the twentieth century.
29. When did someone build the Panama Canal?
30. Did someone build the Panama Canal in the twentieth century?

□ **EXERCISE 13:** Complete the sentences with the correct form of the verbs (active or passive) in parentheses.

1. This book (*have to return*) _____ to the library today.

2. The other books (*return*) _____ yesterday.

3. That book (*should return*) _____ tomorrow.

4. These letters (*be going to mail*) _____ tomorrow.

5. That letter (*ought to send*) _____ immediately.

6. This letter (*must send*) _____ today.

7. Those letters (*arrive*) _____ yesterday.

8. I don't have my car today. It's in the garage. It (*repair*) _____
_____ right now.

9. Kate didn't have her car last week because it was in the garage. While it
(*repair*) _____, she took the bus to work.

10. The mechanic (*repair*) _____ Tina's car last
week.

11. Glass (*make*) _____ from sand.

12. You (*should carry, not*) _____ large sums of
money with you.

13. Large sums of money (*ought to keep*) _____ in
a bank, don't you think?

14. At our high school, the students' grades (*send*) _____
to their parents four times each year.

15. I'm sorry, but the computer job is no longer available. A new computer
programmer (*hire, already*) _____.

16. Household cleaning agents (*must use*) _____
with care. For example, mixing chlorine bleach with ammonia (*can
produce*) _____ toxic gases.

17. What products (*manufacture*) _____ in your
country?

18. Aluminum* is a valuable metal that (*can use*) _____
again and again. Because this metal (*can recycle*) _____
_____, aluminum cans (*should throw away, not*)
_____.

19. Endangered wildlife (*must protect*) _____ from
extinction.

20. People with the moral courage to fight against injustices (*can find*)
_____ in every corner of the world.

Aluminum in American English = *aluminium* in British English.

☐ **EXERCISE 14:** Complete the sentences with any appropriate tense, active or passive, of the verbs in parentheses.

1. In prehistoric times, huge herds of horses (*live*) _____ throughout the Americas. But then, for some unknown reason, they (*disappear*) _____ completely from North and South America. Even though the early horses (*die*) _____ out in the Americas, they (*survive*) _____ in Asia.

2. Long ago, horses (*domesticate*)* _____ by central Asian nomads. At first, horses (*use*) _____ in war and in hunting, and oxen (*use*) _____ for farming. Later, horses also (*become*) _____ farm animals.

3. Horses (*reintroduce*) _____ into the Americas by Spaniards in the early fifteenth century. Spanish explorers (*come*) _____ in ships to the New World with their horses on board.

4. When the explorers (*return*) _____ to Spain, they (*leave*) _____ some of their horses behind. These (*develop*) _____ into wild herds. Native American tribes in the western plains (*begin*) _____ to use horses around 1600. Wild horses (*capture*) _____ and (*tame*) _____ for use in war and in hunting.

5. In the 1800s, there were several million wild horses in North America. By the 1970s, that number had become less than 20,000. The wild horses (*hunt*) _____ and (*kill*) _____ principally for use as pet food. Today in the United States, wild horses (*protect*) _____ by law. They (*can kill, not*) _____ for sport or profit. What is your opinion? (*Should protect, wild horses*) _____ by law?

_____
*People domesticate (tame) animals.

11-8 USING PAST PARTICIPLES AS ADJECTIVES (STATIVE PASSIVE)

BE + ADJECTIVE (a) Paul *is* **young**. (b) Paul *is* **tall**. (c) Paul *is* **hungry**. **BE + PAST PARTICIPLE** (d) Paul *is* **married**. (e) Paul *is* **tired**. (f) Paul *is* **frightened**.	**Be** can be followed by an adjective. The adjective describes or gives information about the subject of the sentence. **Be** can be followed by a past participle (the passive form). The past participle is often like an adjective. The past participle describes or gives information about the subject of the sentence. Past participles are used as adjectives in many common, everyday expressions.
(g) Paul *is married* **to** Susan. (h) Paul *was excited* **about** the game. (i) Paul *will be prepared* **for** the exam.	Often the past participles in these expressions are followed by particular prepositions + an object. For example: • **married** is followed by **to** (+ an object). • **excited** is followed by **about** (+ an object). • **prepared** is followed by **for** (+ an object).

SOME COMMON EXPRESSIONS WITH BE + PAST PARTICIPLE

1. *be acquainted (with)*	13. *be excited (about)*	25. *be opposed (to)*
2. *be bored (with, by)*	14. *be exhausted (from)*	26. *be pleased (with)*
3. *be broken*	15. *be finished (with)*	27. *be prepared (for)*
4. *be closed*	16. *be frightened (of, by)*	28. *be qualified (for)*
5. *be composed of*	17. *be gone (from)*	29. *be related (to)*
6. *be crowded (with)*	18. *be hurt*	30. *be satisfied (with)*
7. *be devoted (to)*	19. *be interested (in)*	31. *be scared (of, by)*
8. *be disappointed (in, with)*	20. *be involved (in)*	32. *be shut*
9. *be divorced (from)*	21. *be located in, south of, etc.*	33. *be spoiled*
10. *be done (with)*	22. *be lost*	34. *be terrified (of, by)*
11. *be drunk (on)*	23. *be made of*	35. *be tired (of, from)**
12. *be engaged (to)*	24. *be married (to)*	36. *be worried (about)*

*I'm **tired of** the cold weather. = *I've had enough cold weather. I want the weather to get warm.*
I'm **tired from** working hard all day. = *I'm exhausted because I worked hard all day.*

☐ **EXERCISE 15:** Complete the sentences with the expressions in the list. Use the SIMPLE PRESENT TENSE.

be acquainted	be exhausted	be related
be broken	be located	be satisfied
be composed	be lost	be scared
be crowded	be made	be spoiled
be disappointed	be qualified	✔be worried

1. Dennis isn't doing well in school this semester. He _____ **is worried** _____

about his grades.

2. My shirt _____ of cotton.

3. I live in a one-room apartment with four other people. Our apartment

_____.

4. Vietnam _____ in Southeast Asia.

5. I'm going to go straight to bed tonight. It's been a hard day. I

_____.

6. I _____ to Jessica Adams. She's my cousin.

7. Excuse me, sir, but I think I _____. Could you

please tell me how to get to the bus station from here?

8. My tape recorder doesn't work. It _____.

9. We leave a light on in our son's bedroom at night because he

_____ of the dark.

10. Alice thinks her boss should pay her more money. She _____

not _____ with her present salary.

11. The children _____. I had promised to take them

to the beach today, but now we can't go because it's raining.

12. _____ you _____ with Mrs. Novinsky?

Have you ever met her?

13. According to the job description, an applicant must have a Master's

degree and at least five years of teaching experience. Unfortunately, I

_____ not _____ for that job.

14. This milk doesn't taste right. I think it _____. I'm

not going to drink it.

15. Water _____ of hydrogen and oxygen.

☐ **EXERCISE 16:** Complete the sentences with appropriate prepositions.

1. The day before Christmas, the stores are crowded __**with**__ last-
minute shoppers.

2. Are you qualified _____ that job?

3. Mr. Heath loves his family very much. He is devoted _____ them.

4. Our dog runs under the bed during storms. He's terrified _____
thunder.

5. My sister is married _____ a law student.

6. Are you prepared _____ the test?

7. I'll be finished _____ my work in another minute or two.

8. Jason is excited _____ going to Hollywood.

9. Ms. Brown is opposed _____ the new tax plan.

10. Jane isn't satisfied _____ her present apartment. She's looking for a new one.

11. I failed the test because I didn't study. I'm disappointed _____ myself.

12. Janet doesn't take good care of herself. I'm worried _____ her health.

13. I'm tired _____ this rainy weather. I hope the sun shines tomorrow.

14. In terms of evolution, a hippopotamus is related _____ a horse.

15. The students are involved _____ many extracurricular activities.

16. Are you acquainted _____ this author? I think her books are excellent.

17. When will you be done _____ your work?

18. I'm starving! Right now I'm interested _____ only one thing: food.

19. The children want some new toys. They're bored _____ their old ones.

20. Sam is engaged _____ his childhood sweetheart.

21. Our daughter is scared _____ dogs.

22. You've done a good job. You should be very pleased _____ yourself.

□ **EXERCISE 17—ORAL (BOOKS CLOSED):** Supply appropriate prepositions + "*someone*" or "*something*."

Example: I'm worried . . . .
Response: about someone/something.

1. I'm interested . . . .
2. I'm married . . . .
3. I'm scared . . . .

4. I'm related . . . .
5. I'm disappointed . . . .
6. I'm qualified . . . .

7. I'm satisfied . . . .
8. I'm prepared . . . .
9. I'm acquainted . . . .
10. I'm opposed . . . .
11. I'm frightened . . . .
12. I'm excited . . . .

13. I'm engaged . . . .
14. I'm worried . . . .
15. I'm tired . . . .
16. I'm finished . . . .
17. I'm done . . . .
18. I'm involved . . . .

Repeat the exercise. Use only the past participles as cues and make your own sentences.

 Example: worried
 Response: I'm worried about my brother./The teacher is worried about my grades./We are worried about the next test./etc.

☐ **EXERCISE 18:** Complete the sentences with the words in parentheses. Use the PASSIVE form, SIMPLE PRESENT or SIMPLE PAST. Include PREPOSITIONS where necessary.

1. (*close*) When we got to the post office, it _____ **was closed** _____ .

2. (*make*) My earrings _____ **are made of** _____ gold.

3. (*divorce*) Sally and Tom were married for six years, but now they
      _____ .

4. (*relate*) Your name is Tom Hood. _____ you _____
      Mary Hood?

5. (*spoil*) This fruit _____. I think I'd better throw it out.

6. (*exhaust*) Last night I _____, so I went straight to bed.

7. (*involve*) Last week I _____ a three-car accident.

8. (*locate*) The University of Washington _____
      Seattle.

9. (*drink*) Ted _____. He's making a fool
      of himself.

10. (*interest*) I _____ learning more about that subject.

11. (*devote*) Linda loves her job. She _____ her work.

12. (*lose*) What's the matter, little boy? _____ you _____?

13. (*terrify*) Once when we were swimming at the beach, we saw a
      shark. All of us _____.

14. (*acquaint*) _____ you _____ Sue's roommate?

15. (*qualify*)   I didn't get the job. The interviewer said that I

_____ not _____ it.

16. (*disappoint*) My son brought home a report card with all D's and F's.

I can't understand it. I _____ him.

17. (*do*)   At last, I _____ my homework. Now I

can go to bed.

18. (*crowd*) There are too many students in our class. The classroom

_____.

19. (*shut*)   It's starting to rain. _____ all of the windows

_____?

20. (*go*)   Where's my wallet? It _____! Did you

take it?

11-9   PARTICIPIAL ADJECTIVES: -*ED* vs. -*ING*

Indian art interests me. (a) I am **interested** in Indian art. 　INCORRECT: I am interesting in Indian art. (b) Indian art is **interesting**. 　INCORRECT: Indian art is interested. **The news surprised Kate.** (c) Kate was **surprised**. (d) The news was **surprising**.	The past participle (-*ed*)★ and the present participle (-*ing*) can be used as adjectives. In (a): The past participle (*interested*) describes how a person feels. In (b): The present participle (*interesting*) describes the **cause** of the feeling. The cause of the interest is Indian art. In (c): "surprised" describes how Kate felt. The past participle carries a passive meaning: *Kate was surprised* **by the news**. In (d): "the news" was the cause of the surprise.

★The past participle of regular verbs ends in -*ed*. Some verbs have irregular forms. See Chart 2-4.

☐ **EXERCISE 19:** Complete the sentences with the -*ed* or -*ing* form of verbs in italics.

1. Greg's classes *interest* him.

   a. Greg's classes are ____**interesting**____.

   b. Greg is an ____**interested**____ student.

2. Jane's classes *bore* her.

   a. Jane's classes are _____.

   b. Jane is a _____ student.

3. Mike heard some bad news. The bad news *depressed* him.

   a. Mike is very sad. In other words, he is _____.

   b. The news made Mike feel sad. The news was _____.

4. The exploration of space *interests* me.

   a. I'm _____ in the exploration of space.

   b. The exploration of space is _____ to me.

5. Nancy's rude behavior *embarrassed* her parents.

   a. Nancy's rude behavior was _____.

   b. Nancy's parents were _____.

6. The nation's leader stole money. The scandal *shocked* the nation.

   a. It was a _____ scandal.

   b. The _____ nation soon replaced the leader.

7. I like to study sea life. The subject of marine biology *fascinates* me.

   a. I'm _____ by marine biology.

   b. Marine biology is a _____ subject.

8. Emily is going to Australia. The idea of going on this trip *excites* her.

   a. Emily is _____ about going on this trip.

   b. She thinks it is going to be an _____ trip.

☐ **EXERCISE 20:** Circle the correct form (*-ing* or *-ed*) of the words in parentheses.

  1. Don't bother to read that book. It's (*boring,* *bored*).

  2. The students are (*interesting, interested*) in learning more about the subject.

  3. Ms. Green doesn't explain things well. The students are (*confusing, confused*).

  4. Have you heard the latest news? It's really (*exciting, excited*).

  5. I don't understand these directions. I'm (*confusing, confused*).

  6. I read an (*interesting, interested*) article in the newspaper this morning.

  7. I heard some (*surprising, surprised*) news on the radio.

  8. I'm (*boring, bored*). Let's do something. How about going to a movie?

  9. Mr. Sawyer bores me. I think he is a (*boring, bored*) person.

 10. Mr. Ball fascinates me. I think he is a (*fascinating, fascinated*) person.

11. Most young children are (*fascinating, fascinated*) by animals.

12. Young children think that animals are (*fascinating, fascinated*).

13. I was very (*embarrassing, embarrassed*) yesterday when I spilled my drink on the dinner table.

14. That was an (*embarrassing, embarrassed*) experience.

15. I read a (*shocking, shocked*) report yesterday on the number of children who die from starvation in the world every day. I was really (*shocking, shocked*).

16. The children went to a circus. For them, the circus was (*exciting, excited*). The (*exciting, excited*) children jumped up and down.

11-10 GET + ADJECTIVE; GET + PAST PARTICIPLE

GET + ADJECTIVE (a) I **am getting hungry**. Let's eat. (b) Eric **got nervous** before the job interview.	**Get** can be followed by an adjective. **Get** gives the idea of change—the idea of becoming, beginning to be, growing to be. In (a): *I'm getting hungry = I wasn't hungry before, but now I'm beginning to be hungry.*
GET + PAST PARTICIPLE (c) I**'m getting tired**. Let's stop working. (d) Steve and Rita **got married** last month.	Sometimes **get** is followed by a past participle. The past participle after **get** is like an adjective; it describes the subject of the sentence.

GET + ADJECTIVE			GET + PAST PARTICIPLE		
get angry	get dry	get quiet	get acquainted	get drunk	get involved
get bald	get fat	get rich	get arrested	get engaged	get killed
get big	get full	get serious	get bored	get excited	get lost
get busy	get hot	get sick	get confused	get finished	get married
get close	get hungry	get sleepy	get crowded	get frightened	get scared
get cold	get interested	get thirsty	get divorced	get hurt	get sunburned
get dark	get late	get well	get done	get interested	get tired
get dirty	get nervous	get wet	get dressed	get invited	get worried
get dizzy	get old				

☐ **EXERCISE 21:** Complete the sentences. Use each word in the list only one time.

angry	confused	hot	married
arrested	dizzy	hungry	rich
bald	dressed	hurt	sick
bored	drunk	late	sleepy
✔cold	full	lost	tired

1. In winter, the weather gets _____*cold*_____.

2. In summer, the weather gets _____.

3. This food is delicious, but I can't eat any more. I'm getting

   _____.

4. I overslept this morning. When I finally woke up, I jumped out of bed,

   got _____, picked up my books, and ran to class.

5. Mom and Dad are going to celebrate their 50th wedding anniversary

   next month. They got _____ fifty years ago.

6. When Jane gave us directions to her house, I got _____.

   So I asked her to explain again how to get there.

7. I didn't understand Jane's directions very well, so on the way to her

   house last night I got _____. I couldn't find her house.

8. Calm down! Take it easy! You shouldn't get _____. It's not good for your blood pressure.

9. Mr. Anderson is losing some of his hair. He's getting _____.

10. I didn't like the movie last night. It wasn't interesting. I got _____ and wanted to leave early.

11. When's dinner? I'm getting _____.

12. We should leave for the concert soon. It's getting _____. We should leave in the next five minutes if we want to be on time.

13. I want to make a lot of money. Do you know a good way to get _____ quick?

14. Jake got _____ for stealing a car yesterday. He is in jail now.

15. Was it a bad accident? Did anyone get _____?

16. When I turned around and around in a circle, I got _____.

17. I don't feel very good. I think I'm getting _____. Maybe I should see a doctor.

18. My friends got _____ at the party Saturday night, so I drove them home in my car. They were in no condition to drive.

19. I think I'll go to bed. I'm getting _____.

20. Let's stop working and take a break. I'm getting _____.

□ **EXERCISE 22:** Complete the sentences with an appropriate form of *get*.

1. Shake a leg! Step on it! _____**Get**_____ busy. There's no time to waste.

2. Tom and Sue _____**got**_____ married last month.

3. Let's stop working for a while. I ____**am getting**____ tired.

4. I don't want _____**to get**_____ old, but I guess it happens to everybody.

5. I _____ interested in biology when I was in high school, so I decided to major in it in college.

6. My father started _____ bald when he was in his twenties. I'm in my twenties, and I'm starting _____ bald. It must be in the genes.

7. Brrr. It _____ cold in here. Maybe we should turn on the furnace.

8. When I was in the hospital, I got a card from my aunt and uncle. It said, "_____ well soon."

9. When I went downtown yesterday, I _____ lost. I didn't remember to take my map of the city with me.

10. A: Why did you leave the party early?
    B: I _____ bored.

11. A: I _____ hungry. Let's eat soon.
    B: Okay.

12. A: What happened?
    B: I don't know. Suddenly I _____ dizzy, but I'm okay now.

13. A: Do you want to go for a walk?
    B: Well, I don't know. It _____ dark outside right now. Let's wait and go for a walk tomorrow.

14. I always _____ nervous when I have to give a speech.

15. A: Where's Bud? He was supposed to be home two hours ago. He always calls when he's late. I _____ worried. Maybe we should call the police.

B: Relax. He'll be home soon.

16. A: Hurry up and _____ dressed. We have to leave in ten minutes.

B: I'm almost ready.

17. A: I'm going on a diet.

B: Oh?

A: See? This shirt is too tight. I _____ fat.

18. A: Janice and I are thinking about _____ married in June.

B: That's a nice month for a wedding.

☐ **EXERCISE 23—ERROR ANALYSIS:** Find and correct the errors in the following sentences.

> *Example:* I am agree with him.
> *Correction:* I agree with him.

1. An accident was happened at the corner yesterday.

2. This is belong to me.

3. I am very surprise by the news.

4. I'm interesting in that subject.

5. He is marry with my cousin.

6. Thailand is locate in Southeast Asia.

7. Mary's dog was died last week.

8. Were you surprise when you saw him?

9. When I went downtown, I get lost.

10. Last night I very tire.

11. The bus was arrived ten minutes late.

12. When are you going to get marry?

13. I am agree with you.

14. We are not agree with him.

11-11 USING *BE USED/ACCUSTOMED TO* AND *GET USED/ACCUSTOMED TO*

(a) I **am used to** hot weather. (b) I **am accustomed to** hot weather. (c) I am used **to living** in a hot climate. (d) I am accustomed **to living** in a hot climate.	(a) and (b) have the same meaning: "Living in a hot climate is usual and normal for me. I'm familiar with what it is like to live in a hot climate. Hot weather isn't strange or different to me." Notice in (c) and (d): **to** (a preposition) is followed by the **-ing** form of a verb (a gerund).★
(e) I just moved from Florida to Alaska. I have never lived in a cold climate before, but I **am getting used to (accustomed to)** the cold weather here.	In (e): *I'm getting used to/accustomed to* = something is beginning to seem usual and normal to me.

★COMPARE: To express the habitual past (see 2-9), the infinitive form follows **used**: *I used to live in Chicago, but now I live in New York.* However, **be used to** is followed by a gerund: *I am used to living in a big city.*
NOTE: In both **used to** (habitual past) and **be used to**, the "d" is not pronounced in "used."

☐ **EXERCISE 24:** Complete the sentences with *be used to*, affirmative or negative.

1. Juan is from Mexico. He _____ **is used to** _____ hot weather. He _____ **isn't used to** ___ cold weather.

2. Alice was born and raised in Chicago. She _____ living in a big city.

3. My hometown is New York City, but this year I'm going to school in a town with a population of 10,000. I _____ living in a small town. I _____ living in a big city.

4. We do a lot of exercises in class. We _____ doing exercises.

*Complete the sentences with **be accustomed to**, affirmative or negative.*
NOTICE: ***accustomed** is spelled with two "c's" and one "m."*

5. Spiro is from Greece. He _____ eating Greek food, but he _____ eating American food.

6. I always get up around 6:00 A.M. I _____ getting up early. I _____ sleeping late.

7. Our teacher always gives us a lot of homework. We _____

_____ having a lot of homework every day.

8. We rarely take multiple choice tests. We _____

taking that kind of test.

☐ **EXERCISE 25—ORAL (BOOKS CLOSED):** Talk about yourself. Use *be used/accustomed to*.

Example: cold weather
Response: I am (OR: I am not) used/accustomed to cold weather.

1. hot weather
2. cold weather
3. living in a warm climate
4. living in a cold climate
5. living in a big city
6. living in a small town
7. getting up early
8. sleeping late
9. eating a big breakfast
10. drinking coffee in the morning
11. (American) food
12. being on my own*

☐ **EXERCISE 26—ORAL (BOOKS CLOSED):**   Answer the questions.

Example: What time are you accustomed to getting up?
Response: I'm accustomed to getting up (at 7:30).

1. What time are you accustomed to getting up?
2. What time are you used to going to bed?
3. Are you accustomed to living in (*name of this city*)?
4. Are you accustomed to living in a big city?
5. Are you used to speaking English every day?
6. Who lives with a roommate? Are you accustomed to that?
7. Who lives alone? Are you accustomed to that?
8. What are you accustomed to eating for breakfast?
9. Our weather right now is hot/cold/humid/cold and wet/etc. Are you used to this kind of weather?
10. How are you used to getting to school every day?
11. Where are you accustomed to eating lunch?
12. What time are you accustomed to eating dinner?
13. What kind of food are you accustomed to eating?
14. Who lives in a dorm? Are you used to the noise in a dorm?
15. Are you used to speaking English everyday, or does it seem strange to you?

_____

To be on one's own is an idiom. It means to be away from one's family and responsible for oneself.

□ **EXERCISE 27:** You are living in a new place (country, city, apartment, dorm, etc.) and going to a new school. What adjustments have you had to make? Write about them by completing the sentences with your own words.

1. I'm getting used to _____

2. I'm also getting accustomed to _____

3. I have gotten accustomed to _____

4. I haven't gotten used to _____

5. I can't get used to _____

6. Do you think I will ever get accustomed to _____

11-12 USING *BE SUPPOSED TO*

(a) Mike *is supposed to call* me tomorrow. (IDEA: I expect Mike to call me tomorrow.) (b) We *are supposed to write* a composition. (IDEA: The teacher expects us to write a composition). (c) It *is supposed to rain* today. (IDEA: People expect it to rain today.) (d) Alice *was supposed to be* home at ten. (IDEA: Someone expected Alice to be home at ten.)	*Be supposed to* is used to talk about an activity or event that is expected to occur. In (a): The idea of *is supposed to* is that Mike is expected (by me) to call. I asked him to call me. He promised to call me. I expect him to call me. NOTE: The present form of *be* is used for both future expectations and present expectations.

□ **EXERCISE 28—ORAL:** Make sentences with a similar meaning by using *be supposed to.*

1. The teacher expects us to be on time for class.
   → *We are supposed to be on time for class.*
2. People expect the weather to be cold tomorrow.
3. People expect the plane to arrive at 6:00.
4. I expect Tom to call me.
5. My boss expects me to work late tonight.
6. I expect the mail to arrive at noon.
7. Someone expected me to return this book to the library yesterday, but I didn't.
8. Our professor expects us to read Chapter 9 before class tomorrow.
9. Someone expected me to go to a party last night, but I stayed home.
10. The teacher expects us to do Exercise 10 for homework.
11. The weather bureau has predicted rain for tomorrow. According to the weather bureau, it . . . .

12. The directions on the pill bottle say, "Take one pill every six hours." According to the directions on the bottle, I . . . .

13. My mother expects me to dust the furniture and (to) vacuum the carpet.

☐ **EXERCISE 29—ORAL:** Read the dialogues and then answer the questions. Use *be supposed to.*

1. TOM'S BOSS: Mail this package.
   TOM: Yes, sir.
   What is Tom supposed to do?
   →*He is supposed to mail a package.*

2. MARY: Call me at nine.
   ANN: Okay.
   What is Ann supposed to do?

3. MS. MARTINEZ: Please make your bed before you go to school.
   JOHNNY: Okay, Mom.
   What is Johnny supposed to do?

4. MR. TAKADA: Put your dirty clothes in the laundry basket.
   SUSIE: Okay, Dad
   What is Susie supposed to do?

5. MRS. WILSON: Bobby, pick up your toys and put them away.
   BOBBY: Okay, Mom.
   MRS. WILSON: Annie, please hang up your coat.
   ANNIE: Okay, Mom.
   What are the children supposed to do?

6. DR. KETTLE: You should take one pill every eight hours.
   PATIENT: All right, Dr. Kettle. Anything else?
   DR. KETTLE: Drink plenty of fluids.
   What is the patient supposed to do?

7. PROF. LARSON: Read Chapter 10 and answer the questions at the end of the chapter.
   STUDENTS: (no response)
   What are the students supposed to do?

8. PROF. THOMPSON: Read the directions carefully, use a No. 2 pencil, and raise your hand if you have any questions.
   STUDENTS: (no response)
   What are the students supposed to do?

☐ **EXERCISE 30—WRITTEN:** Describe how a particular holiday is celebrated in your country. What is done in the morning, the afternoon, the evening? What are some of the things that people typically do on this holiday? NOTE: Many of your sentences will be active, but some of them should be passive.

CHAPTER *12*
Adjective Clauses

12-1 ADJECTIVE CLAUSES: INTRODUCTION

ADJECTIVES	ADJECTIVE CLAUSES*
An **adjective** modifies a noun. "*Modify*" means to change a little. An adjective gives a little different meaning to a noun. It describes or gives information about a noun. (See Chart 4-4).	An **adjective clause** modifies a noun. It describes or gives information about a noun.
An adjective usually comes in front of a noun.	An adjective clause follows a noun.
(a) I met a [*adjective* **kind**] + [*noun* man.] (b) I met a [*adjective* **famous**] + [*noun* man.]	(c) I met a [*noun* man] + [*adjective clause* **who is kind to everybody.**] (d) I met a [*noun* man] + [*adjective clause* **who is a famous poet.**] (e) I met a [*noun* man] + [*adjective clause* **who lives in Chicago.**]

*Grammar terminology:
A **clause** is a structure that has a subject and a verb.
There are two kinds of clauses: independent and dependent. An **independent clause** is a main clause. It can stand alone as a sentence. A **dependent clause** must be connected to an independent clause. A dependent clause cannot stand alone as a sentence. An adjective clause is a dependent clause.

 I met a man = *an independent clause*
 who is kind to everybody = *a dependent clause*

12-2 USING *WHO* AND *WHOM* IN ADJECTIVE CLAUSES

(a) The man is friendly.	**S V** **He** lives next to me. ↓ **who** ↓ **S V** **who** lives next to me	In (a): **He** is a subject pronoun. **He** refers to "the man." To make an adjective clause, we can change **he** to **who**. **Who** is a subject pronoun. **Who** refers to "the man."
(b) The man **who lives next to me** is friendly.		In (b): An adjective clause immediately follows the noun it modifies. INCORRECT: *The man is friendly who lives next to me.*
(c) The man was friendly.	**S V O** I met **him**. ↓ **whom** **O S V** **whom** I met	In (c): **Him** is an object pronoun. **Him** refers to the "the man." To make an adjective clause, we can change **him** to **whom**. **Whom** is an object pronoun. **Whom** refers to "the man."* **Whom** comes at the beginning of an adjective clause.
(d) The man **whom I met** was friendly.		In (d): An adjective clause immediately follows the noun it modifies. INCORRECT: *The man was friendly whom I met.*

*In informal English, **who** is often used as an object pronoun instead of **whom**:
    FORMAL: *The man **whom** I met was friendly.*
    INFORMAL: *The man **who** I met was friendly.*

☐ **EXERCISE 1:** Combine the two sentences into one sentence. Make "b." an adjective clause. Use **who** or **whom**.

1. a. Do you know the people?   b. They live in the white house.

    → *Do you know the people who live in the white house?*

2. a. The woman gave me some information.   b. I called her.

    → *The woman whom I called gave me some information.*

3. a. The police officer was friendly.   b. He gave me directions.

4. a. The waitress was friendly.   b. She served us dinner.

5. a. I don't know the man.   b. He is talking to Rita.

6. a. The people were very nice.   b. I met them at the party last night.

7. a. The woman thanked me.   b. I helped her.

8. a. Do you like the mechanic?   b. He fixed your car.

9. a. Mr. Polanski is a mechanic.   b. You can trust this mechanic.

10. a. The people have three cars.   b. They live next to me.

11. a. I talked to the woman.   b. She was sitting next to me.

12. a. I talked to the people.   b. They were sitting next to me.

13. a. The woman was walking her dog.   b. I saw her.

14. a. The people were playing football.   b. I saw them at the park.

□ **EXERCISE 2:** Complete the sentences in Column A with the adjective clauses in Column B. Consult your dictionary if necessary.

Example: A Bostonian is someone who lives in Boston.

COLUMN A

1. A Bostonian is someone . . . .

2. A pilot is a person . . . .

3. A procrastinator is someone . . . .

4. A botanist is a scientist . . . .

5. An insomniac is somebody . . . .

6. A revolutionary is someone . . . .

7. A misanthrope is a person . . . .

8. A meteorologist is a person . . . .

9. A jack-of-all-trades is someone . . . .

10. An expert can be defined as a person . . . .

COLUMN B

a. who has trouble sleeping.

b. who seeks to overthrow the government.

c. who flies an airplane.

d. who studies weather phenomena.

e. who lives in Boston.

f. who hates people.

g. who always puts off doing things.

h. who has special knowledge in one area.

i. who has many skills.

j. who studies plants.

□ **EXERCISE 3:** Complete the sentences with your own words. Consult your dictionary if necessary.

1. A baker is a person who _____

2. A mechanic is someone who _____

3. A bartender is a person who _____

4. A philatelist is someone who _____

5. A spendthrift is somebody who _____

6. An astronomer is a scientist who _____

7. A carpenter is a person who _____

8. A miser is someone who _____

12-3 USING *WHO*, *WHOM*, AND *THAT* IN ADJECTIVE CLAUSES

(a) The man is friendly. **He** [↓ who / that] lives next to me. (b) The man **who** *lives next to me* is friendly. (c) The man **that** *lives next to me* is friendly.	In addition to **who**, we can use **that** as the subject of an adjective clause. (b) and (c) have the same meaning.
	A subject pronoun cannot be omitted: INCORRECT: *The man lives next to me is friendly.* CORRECT: *The man who/that lives next to me is friendly.*
(d) The man was friendly. I met **him.** [↓ whom / that] (e) The man **whom** *I met* was friendly. (f) The man **that** *I met* was friendly. (g) The man **Ø** *I met* was friendly.	In addition to **whom**, we can use **that** as the object in an adjective clause. (e) and (f) have the same meaning.
	An object pronoun can be omitted from an adjective clause. (e), (f), and (g) have the same meaning. In (g): The symbol "Ø" means "nothing goes here."

☐ **EXERCISE 4:** Change *that* to *who* or *who(m)*.★ Also, omit *that* if possible.

1. The woman that I met last night was interesting.
    → *The woman who(m) I met last night was interesting.*
    → *The woman Ø I met last night was interesting.*

2. The man that answered the phone was polite.

3. The people that Ann is visiting live on Elm Street.

4. Do you like the boy that is talking to Jennifer?

5. The students that came to class late missed the quiz.

6. I didn't know any of the people that Bill invited to his party.

7. The woman that I saw in the park was feeding the pigeons.

8. The woman that was feeding the pigeons had a sackful of bread crumbs.

9. I like the barber that usually cuts my hair.

10. The person that I admire most is my grandmother.

★The parentheses around the "m" in *who(m)* indicate that sometimes (in everyday informal usage) *who* is used as an object pronoun instead of *whom*.

12-4 USING *WHICH* AND *THAT* IN ADJECTIVE CLAUSES

(a) The river is polluted. **S** **V** **It** flows through town. ↓ **which** **that**	**Who** and **whom** refer to people. **Which** refers to things. **That** can refer to either people or things.
(b) The river **which** *flows through town* is polluted. (c) The river **that** *flows through town* is polluted.	In (a): To make an adjective clause, we can change **it** to **which** or **that**. **It**, **which**, and **that** all refer to a thing (the river). (b) and (c) have the same meaning.
	When **which** and **that** are used as the subject of an adjective clause, they CANNOT be omitted.
(d) The books were expensive. I bought **them**. ↓ **which** **that**	**Which** or **that** can be used as an object in an adjective clause, as in (e) and (f).
(e) The books **which** *I bought* were expensive. (f) The books **that** *I bought* were expensive. (g) The books **Ø** *I bought* were expensive.	An object pronoun can be omitted from an adjective clause, as in (g). (e), (f) and (g) have the same meaning.

☐ **EXERCISE 5:** Combine the two sentences into one sentence. Make "b." an adjective clause. Give all the possible forms.

1. a. The pill made me sleepy.   b. I took it.
   → *The pill which I took made me sleepy.*
   → *The pill that I took made me sleepy.*
   → *The pill Ø I took made me sleepy.*

2. a. The soup was too salty.   b. I had it for lunch.

3. a. I have a class.   b. It begins at 8:00 A.M.

4. a. I know a man.   b. He doesn't have to work for a living.

5. a. My daughter asked me a question.   b. I couldn't answer it.

6. a. All of the people can come.   b. I asked them to my party.

7. a. I lost the scarf.   b. I borrowed it from my roommate.

8. a. A lion is an animal.   b. This animal lives in Africa.

9. a. A globe is a ball.   b. This ball has a map of the world on it.

10. a. Where can I catch the bus?   b. It goes downtown.

11. a. The bus is always crowded.   b. I take it to school every morning.

12. a. The woman predicted my future.   b. She read my palm.

13. a. I have some valuable antiques.   b. I found them in my
                                          grandmother's attic.

14. a. The notes helped me a lot.   b. I borrowed them from you.

□ **EXERCISE 6:** Complete the sentences in Column A with the adjective clauses in Column B.

Example: A quart is a liquid measure that equals two pints.

COLUMN A

1. A quart is a liquid measure . . . .
2. A puzzle is a problem . . . .
3. Cake is a dessert . . . .
4. A passport is a special paper . . . .
5. A hammer is a tool . . . .
6. A barometer is an instrument . . . .
7. A coin is a piece of metal . . . .
8. A pyramid is a structure . . . .

COLUMN B

a. that is difficult to solve.
b. that measures air pressure.
✔c. that equals two pints.
d. that is used to pound nails.
e. that is square at the bottom and has four sides
   that come together at the top in a point.
f. that is used as money.
g. that permits a citizen to travel in other
   countries.
h. that is made of flour, eggs, milk, and sugar.

12-5 SINGULAR AND PLURAL VERBS IN ADJECTIVE CLAUSES

(a) I know **the man** *who **is** sitting over there.*	In (a): The verb in the adjective clause (**is**) is singular because **who** refers to a singular noun, "man."
(b) I know **the people** *who **are** sitting over there.*	In (b): The verb in the adjective clause (**are**) is plural because **who** refers to a plural noun, "people."

☐ **EXERCISE 7:** Circle the correct word in parentheses.

1. The students who (*is, are*) in my class come from many countries.

2. I met some people who (*knows, know*) my brother.

3. The student who (*is, are*) talking to the teacher is from Peru.

4. I talked to the men who (*was, were*) sitting near me.

5. Do you know the people that (*lives, live*) in that house?

6. Biographies are books which (*tells, tell*) the stories of people's lives.

7. A book that (*tells, tell*) the story of a person's life is called a biography.

8. The woman that (*was, were*) sitting in front of me at the movie was wearing a big hat.

9. The people who (*was, were*) standing in line to get into the theater were cold and wet.

10. Water is a chemical compound that (*consists, consist*) of oxygen and hydrogen.

11. There are two students in my class who (*speaks, speak*) Portuguese.

12. Cedar waxwings are gray-brown birds that (*lives, live*) in most parts of North America. If you see a crested bird that (*is, are*) a little larger than a sparrow and (*has, have*) a band of yellow across the end of its tail, it may be a cedar waxwing.

13. The heart of education is in a culture's literature. People who (*reads, read*) gain not only knowledge but also pleasure. A person who (*does, do*) not read is no better off than a person who cannot read.

12-6 USING PREPOSITIONS IN ADJECTIVE CLAUSES

(a) The man was helpful.		I talked **PREP** *to* **Obj.** *him*.	

	Obj.	**PREP**	
(b) The man	*whom I talked to*		was helpful.
(c) The man	*that I talked to*		was helpful.
(d) The man	Ø *I talked to*		was helpful.

	PREP	**Obj.**	
(e) The man	*to*	*whom I talked*	was helpful.

Whom, **which**, and **that** can be used as the object of a preposition in an adjective clause.
REMINDER: An object pronoun can be omitted from an adjective clause, as in (d) and (i).

In very formal English, a preposition often comes at the beginning of an adjective clause, as in (e) and (j). The preposition is followed by either **whom** or **which** (not **that**) and the pronoun CANNOT be omitted.

(b), (c), (d), and (e) have the same meaning.

(f) The chair is hard.		I am sitting **PREP** *in* **Obj.** *it*.	

	Obj.	**PREP**	
(g) The chair	*which I am sitting in*		is hard.
(h) The chair	*that I am sitting in*		is hard.
(i) The chair	Ø *I am sitting in*		is hard.

	PREP	**Obj.**	
(j) The chair	*in*	*which I am sitting*	is hard.

(g), (h), (i), and (j) have the same meaning.

☐ **EXERCISE 8:** Combine the two sentences in each pair. Use "b." as an adjective clause. Give all the possible forms of the adjective clauses.

1. a. The movie was interesting.
   b. We went to it.
   → *The movie which we went to was interesting.*
   → *The movie that we went to was interesting.*
   → *The movie Ø we went to was interesting.*
   → *The movie to which we went was interesting.*

2. a. The woman pays me a fair salary.
   b. I work for her.

3. a. The man is over there.
   b. I told you about him.

4. a. I want to tell you about the party.
   b. I went to it last night.

5. a. The person is sitting at that desk.
   b. You should talk to her about your problem.

6. a. Alicia likes the family.

    b. She is living with them.

7. a. The picture is beautiful.

    b. Tom is looking at it.

8. a. I enjoyed the music.

    b. We listened to it after dinner.

☐ **EXERCISE 9—ORAL:** Combine the sentences, using the second sentence as an adjective clause. Practice omitting the object pronoun (*whom, which, that*).

> *Example:* The hill was steep. I climbed it.
> *Response:* The hill I climbed was steep.

1. I met the people. You told me about them.

2. The bananas were too ripe. My husband bought them.

3. The market has fresh vegetables. I usually go to it.

4. I couldn't understand the woman. I talked to her on the phone.

5. The scrambled eggs were cold. I had them for breakfast at the cafeteria.

6. The office is on Main Street. Amy works in it.

7. I had a good time on the trip. I took it to Glacier National Park.

8. The blouse is made of silk. Mary is wearing it.

9. The doctor prescribed some medicine for my sore throat. I went to him yesterday.

10. The cream was spoiled. I put it in my coffee.

11. The fast-forward button on the tape recorder doesn't work. I bought it last month.

12. Here is the brochure. You asked me about it.

13. The man is tall, dark, and handsome. My sister goes out with him.

14. The university is in New York. I want to go to it.

15. The plane leaves at 7:08 P.M. I'm taking it to Denver.

16. I'm going to call about the want ad. I saw it in last night's paper.

12-7 USING *WHOSE* IN ADJECTIVE CLAUSES

(a) The man called the police. $\boxed{\textbf{\textit{His car}}}$ was stolen. whose car	**Whose*** shows possession. In (a): We can change **his car** to **whose car** to make an adjective clause.
(b) The man **whose car** *was stolen* called the police.	In (b): *whose car was stolen* = an adjective clause.
(c) I know a girl. $\boxed{\textbf{\textit{Her brother}}}$ is a movie star. **whose brother** (d) I know a girl **whose brother** *is a movie star.*	In (c): We can change *her brother* to *whose brother* to make an adjective clause.
(e) The people were friendly. We bought $\boxed{\textit{their house.}}$ **whose house** (f) The people **whose house** *we bought* were friendly.	In (e): We can change *their house* to *whose house* to make an adjective clause.

***Whose** and **who's** have the same pronunciation but NOT the same meaning.

Who's = **who is**: *Who's (who is) your teacher?*

□ **EXERCISE 10:** Combine the two sentences into one sentence. Make "b." an adjective clause. Use **whose**. Situation: You and your friend are at a party. You are telling your friend about the people at the party.

1. a. There is the man.   b. His car was stolen.
   → *There is the man whose car was stolen.*

2. a. There is the woman.   b. Her cat died.

3. a. Over there is the man.   b. I'm dating his daughter.

4. a. Over there is the woman.   b. You met her husband yesterday.

5. a. There is the professor.   b. I'm taking her course.

6. a. That is the man.   b. His son is an astronaut.

7. a. That is the girl.   b. I borrowed her camera.

8. a. There is the boy.   b. His mother is a famous musician.

9. a. They are the people.   b. We visited their house last month.

10. a. That is the couple.   b. Their apartment was burglarized.

☐ EXERCISE 11—ORAL: Combine the sentences. Use *whose.*

       Example: The man called the police. His car was stolen.
       Response: The man whose car was stolen called the police.

1. The woman was sad. Her cat died.

2. The man is friendly. I'm dating his daughter.

3. The woman is my teacher. You met her husband.

4. The professor gives hard tests. I'm taking her course.

5. The man is very proud. His daughter is an astronaut.

6. The girl is a good friend of mine. I borrowed her camera.

7. The boy wants to be a violinist. His mother is a famous musician.

8. The people were very nice. We visited their house.

9. The couple bought new locks. Their apartment was burglarized.

10. I have a friend. Her brother is a police officer.

11. I have a neighbor. His dog barks all day long.

12. I like the people. We went to their house.

13. I thanked the woman. I borrowed her dictionary.

14. The woman shouted "Stop, thief!" Her purse was stolen.

15. The man is famous. His picture is in the newspaper.

☐ EXERCISE 12: Complete the following sentences with *who, whom, which, whose,* or
that. Discuss all the possible completions. Discuss the possibility of omitting
the pronoun.

1. People _____*who* OR: *that*_____ live in New York City are called New

    Yorkers.

2. Tina likes the present ___*which* OR: *that* OR: Ø___ I gave her for her

    birthday.

3. George Washington is the president _____ picture

    is on a one-dollar bill.

4. I like the people with _____ I work.

5. Have you seen the movie _____ is playing at the Fox Theater?

6. A stenographer is a person _____ can write shorthand.

7. Do you know the woman _____ Michael is engaged to?

8. I have a friend _____ father is a famous artist.

9. The camera _____ I bought has a zoom lens.

10. Students _____ have part-time jobs have to budget their time very carefully.

11. The person to _____ you should send your application is the Director of Admissions.

12. That's Tom Jenkins. He's the boy _____ parents live in Switzerland.

13. A thermometer is an instrument _____ measures the temperature.

14. A high-strung person is someone _____ is always nervous.

15. The man _____ I told you about is standing over there.

16. Monkeys will eat eggs, grass, fruit, birds, snakes, insects, nuts, flowers, leaves, and frogs. Monkeys will eat almost anything _____ they can find.

□ **EXERCISE 13—ORAL (BOOKS CLOSED):** Add adjective clauses to the main sentence.

I. MAIN SENTENCE: The man was nice. (*written on the board*)

Example: I met him yesterday.
Response: The man (whom/that) I met yesterday was nice.

1. You introduced me to him.
2. He helped me yesterday.

3. I spoke to him on the phone.
4. I called him.
5. He answered the phone.
6. I had dinner with him last week.
7. He opened the door for me.
8. I told you about him.
9. (. . .) went to a movie with him last night.
10. He gave me directions to the post office.
11. (. . .) roomed with him.
12. He visited our class yesterday.
13. We visited his house.
14. He helped us at the hardware store.
15. I borrowed his pen.
16. I met him at the party last night.

II. MAIN SENTENCE: Do you know the woman? (*written on the board*)

Example: She is standing over there.
Response: Do you know the woman who/that is standing over there?

1. (. . .) is talking to her.
2. Her car was stolen.
3. (. . .) is going to marry her.
4. (. . .) is talking about her.
5. She is waving at us.
6. Her apartment was burglarized.
7. She works in that office.
8. She is sitting over there.
9. My brother is engaged to her.
10. Her son was arrested by the police.

III. MAIN SENTENCE: The movie was good. (*written on the board*)

Example: I saw it yesterday.
Response: The movie (which/that) I saw yesterday was good.

1. We went to it.
2. I watched it on TV last night.
3. (. . .) told me about it.
4. It was playing at (*name of a local theater*).
5. (. . .) saw it.
6. It starred (*name of an actor/actress*).

☐ EXERCISE 14—ERROR ANALYSIS: All of the following sentences contain mistakes. Can you find the mistakes and correct them?

1. The book which I bought it at the bookstore was very expensive.

2. The woman was nice that I met yesterday.

3. The people which live next to me are friendly.

4. I met a woman who her husband is a famous lawyer.

5. Do you know the people who lives in that house?

6. The professor teaches Chemistry 101 is very good.

7. I wrote a thank-you note to the people who I visited their house on Thanksgiving Day.

8. The people who I met them at the party last night were interesting.

9. I enjoyed the music which we listened to it.

10. The man was very angry whose bicycle was stolen.

☐ EXERCISE 15: Underline the adjective clause and complete the sentence with your own words.

1. One of the things I like best _____ **is★ hot and spicy food** _____

2. One of the places I want to visit someday _____

3. One of the people I admire most _____

4. Some of the cities I would like to visit _____ **are★** _____

5. Some of the places I hope to visit someday _____

   _____

6. One of the cities I would like to visit while I'm in this country _____

   _____

7. One of the programs my roommate likes to watch on TV _____

   _____

8. One of the subjects I would like to know more about _____

   _____

★**One of the** + plural noun (+ adjective clause) + **singular** verb.
Some of the + plural noun (+ adjective clause) + **plural** verb.

9. Some of the things I like most in life _____
_____

10. One of the best books I've ever read _____

11. One of the hardest classes I've ever taken _____

12. One of the most fascinating people I've ever met _____
_____

☐ **EXERCISE 16—WRITTEN:** Complete the sentences with your own words. (Use your own paper.)

1. My friend knows a man who . . . .
2. I have a friend whose . . . .
3. I returned the book that . . . .
4. The person who . . . .
5. The people I . . . .
6. The movie we . . . .
7. The people whose . . . .
8. Do you know the woman who . . . ?
9. The book I . . . .
10. The person to whom . . . .
11. One of the places I . . . .
12. Some of the things I . . . .

☐ **EXERCISE 17—WRITTEN:** Imagine that you are in a room full of people. You know everyone who is there. I (your reader) know no one. Tell me who these people are. Write your description of these people. Practice using adjective clauses.

Begin your composition with: *I'm glad you came. Let me tell you about the people who are here. The woman who . . . .*

12-8 MORE PHRASAL VERBS (SEPARABLE)*

cross out	*draw a line through*
do over	*do again*
fill in	*complete a sentence by writing in a blank*
fill out	*write information in a form (e.g., an application form)*
fill up	*fill completely with gas, water, coffee, etc.*
find out	*discover information*
give up	*quit doing something or quit trying*
leave out	*omit*
start over	*start again*
tear down	*destroy a building*
tear off	*detach, tear along a dotted or perforated line*
tear out of	*remove a piece of paper from a book or notebook*
tear up	*tear into small pieces*

*See 9-8 and 9-9 for more information about phrasal verbs.

☐ **EXERCISE 18:** Complete the phrasal verbs.

1. Maria Alvarez's name is supposed to be on this list, but it isn't.
   Someone probably left it _____ by mistake.

2. I can't solve this math problem. I give _____.

3. I'm not satisfied with my composition. I think I'll do it _____.

4. Dick had trouble figuring out what to say in his letter to his girlfriend.
   He started the letter _____ three times.

5. A: Good news! I've been accepted at the University of Tennessee.

   B: Great. When did you find _____?

   A: I got a letter in the mail today.

6. A: My roommate moved last week. Before he left, he filled out a
   change-of-address card at the post office, but I'm still getting some
   of his mail. What should I do?

   B: Cross _____ the old address on a letter and write in his new
   one. Also write "please forward" on the letter. You don't have to use
   another stamp.

7. How much does it cost to fill _____ your gas tank?

8. We're doing an exercise. We're filling _____ blanks with
   prepositions.

9. When I went to Dr. Green's office for the first time, I had to fill
   _____ a long form about my health history.

10. I made a mistake on the check I was writing, so I tore it _____ and
    wrote another check.

11. An old building was in the way of the new highway through the city, so
    they tore the old building _____.

12. John tore a piece of paper _____ _____ his spiral notebook.

13. When I pay my MasterCard bill, I have to tear _____ the top
    portion of the bill along the perforated line and send it back with my
    check.

12-9 MORE PHRASAL VERBS (NONSEPARABLE)*

(a) Last night some friends **dropped in**.	In (a): **drop in** is not followed by an object.
(b) Let's **drop in on** *Alice* this afternoon. Let's **drop in on** *her* this afternoon.	In (b): **drop in on** is followed by an object.
	Some phrasal verbs are three-word verbs when they are followed by an object. These verbs are nonseparable.

drop in (on) . . . . *visit without calling first or without an invitation*
drop out (of) . . . . *stop attending (school)*
fool around (with) . . . . . . *have fun while wasting time*
get along (with) . . . . *have a good relationship with*
get back (from) . . . . *return from (a trip)*
get through (with) . . . . . . *finish*
grow up (in) . . . . *become an adult*
look out (for) . . . . *be careful*
run out (of) . . . . *finish the supply of (something)*
watch out (for) . . . . *be careful*

*See 9-8 and 9-9 for more information about phrasal verbs.

☐ **EXERCISE 19:** Complete the phrasal verbs.

1. Look ___**out**___! There's a car coming!

2. Look ___**out**___ ___**for**___ that car!

3. Where did you grow _____?

4. I grew _____ _____ Springfield.

5. I couldn't finish the examination. I ran _____ _____ time.

6. A: What did you do yesterday?

   B: Nothing much. I just fooled _____.

7. A: Hi, Chris! What's up? I haven't seen you in a long time. Where have you been?

   B: I went to California last week to visit my brother.

   A: Oh? When did you get _____ _____ California?

   B: Just yesterday.

8. A: Where's Jack? He hasn't been in class for at least two weeks.

   B: He dropped _____ _____ school.

9. A: Watch _____ _____ that truck!

   B: What truck?

10. A: What time do you expect to get _____ _____ your
    homework?

    B: In about an hour, as soon as I finish reading this chapter.

11. A: I haven't seen the Grants for a long time. Let's drop

    _____ _____ them this evening.

    B: We'd better call first. They may not like unexpected company.

12. A: I want to change my room in the dorm.

    B: Why?

    A: I don't get _____ _____ my roommate.

CHAPTER 13
Comparisons

☐ **EXERCISE 1—ORAL:** Use the given words to make comparisons.

   1. short/long lines (Compare the lengths of the lines.)

       line A _____

       line B _____

       line C _____

       line D _____

       line E _____

      → *Line C is shorter than lines A and B.*

      → *B is the longest line of all.*

      → *C isn't as long as A.*

      → *(continue to make comparisons)*

   2. happy/sad look on his face

     DAVID   MIKE   RICK   JIM

   3. large/small country (in total land area)

     Brazil: 3,286,488 sq. mi. (8,511,965 sq km)

     Egypt: 385,229 sq. mi. (997,739 sq km)

     Spain: 194,897 sq. mi. (504,782 sq km)

     Canada: 3,553,303 sq. mi. (9,203,054 sq km)

4. easy/difficult question

   FIRST QUESTION: What's 2 plus 2?
   SECOND QUESTION: What's the square root of 937 divided by 16?
   THIRD QUESTION: What's 3 times 127?
   FOURTH QUESTION: What's 2 plus 3?

5. good/bad handwriting

   EXAMPLE A: *The meeting shine at eight!*

   EXAMPLE B: *The meeting starts at eight*

   EXAMPLE C: *The meeting starts at eight!*

13-1 MAKING COMPARISONS WITH *AS . . . AS*

(a) Tina is 21 years old. Sam is also 21.
   Tina is **as old as** Sam (is).
 	
(b) Mike came **as quickly as** he could.
	As . . . as is used to say that the two parts of a comparison are equal or the same in some way.
	   In (a): **as** + *adjective* + **as**
	   In (b): **as** + *adverb* + **as**

(c) Ted is 20. Tina is 21. Ted is **not as old as** Tina. (d) Ted is**n't quite as old as** Tina. (e) Amy is 5. She is**n't nearly as old as** Tina.	Negative form: **not as . . . as.*** **Quite** and **nearly** are often used with the negative: In (d): **not quite as . . . as** = a small difference. In (e): **not nearly as . . . as** = a big difference.
(f) Sam is **just as** *old* **as** Tina. (g) Ted is **nearly/almost as** *old* **as** Tina.	Common modifiers of **as . . . as** are **just** (meaning "exactly") and **nearly/almost**.

*Also possible: **not so . . . as**: *Ted is **not so old as** Tina.*

TINA
age 21

SAM
age 21

TED
age 20

AMY
age 5

☐ **EXERCISE 2—ORAL:** Make comparisons using *as . . . as*.

1. Rita is very busy. Jason is very busy.
   →Rita is . . . *(just) as busy as Jason (is).*
2. Rita is not very busy at all. Jason is very, very busy.
   → Rita isn't . . . *(nearly) as busy as Jason (is).*

3. I was very tired. Susan was very tired. → I was . . . .
4. Adam wasn't tired at all. Susan was very tired. → Adam wasn't . . . .
5. My apartment has two rooms. Po's apartment has two rooms. (use *big*)
6. My apartment has two rooms. Ali's apartment has three rooms. (use *big*)
7. My apartment has two rooms. Anna's apartment has six rooms. (use *big*)
8. Compare the fullness of the glasses. (use *full*)

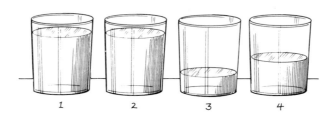

☐ **EXERCISE 3:** Using the given words, complete the sentences with *as . . . as*. Use a
negative verb if appropriate.

1. *a housefly/an ant* __**An ant isn't (quite) as**__ big as ____**a housefly**____ .

2. *honey/sugar* ____**Honey is (just) as**____ sweet as ____**sugar.**____ .

3. *health/money* _____ important as _____ .

4. *adults/children* _____ patient as _____ .

5. *a lake/a sea* _____ big as _____ .

6. *a lion/a tiger* _____ dangerous and wild as _____ .

7. *a galaxy/a solar system* _____ large as _____ .

8. *the Atlantic Ocean/the Pacific Ocean*★ _____ deep as

_____ .

9. *monkeys/people* _____ agile in climbing trees as

_____ .

10. *reading a novel/listening to music*   In my opinion, _____

_____ relaxing as _____ .

11. *a mother/a father*   I think that _____ important

in raising children as _____ .

────────────
★Maximum depths: Atlantic = approx. 30,000 feet/9000 meters.
                Pacific = approx. 36,000 feet/11,000 meters.

☐ **EXERCISE 4:** Complete the sentences by using *as . . . as*.

1. I need you right away! Please come . . . ***as soon as possible.***

2. We can't go any farther. This is . . . ***as far as we can go.***

3. I can't work any faster. I'm working . . . .

4. An orange is sweeter than a lemon. In other words, an orange is not . . . .

5. A stream is usually much narrower than a river. In other words, ...

6. I had expected the test to be difficult, and it was. In other words, the test was just . . . .

7. It's important to use your English every day. You should practice speaking English . . . .

8. You're only old if you feel old. You are . . . young . . . .

9. You might think it's easy to do, but it's not quite . . . .

10. It takes an hour to drive to the airport. It takes an hour to fly to Chicago. In other words, it takes . . . .

☐ **EXERCISE 5:** *As . . . as* is used in many traditional phrases. These phrases are generally spoken rather than written. See how many of these phrases you're familiar with by completing the sentences with the given words.

> ✔ *a bear*   *the hills*   *a pin*
> *a beet*   *a kite*   *a rock*
> *a bird*   *a mule*   *a wet hen*
> *a bull/an ox*

1. When will dinner be ready? I'm as hungry as _____***a bear***_____ !

2. Did Bill really lift that heavy box all by himself? He must be as strong as _____.

3. It was a lovely summer day. School was out, and there was nothing in particular that I had to do. I felt as free as _____.

4. Jeremy won't change his mind. He's as stubborn as _____.

5. Was she angry? You'd better believe it! She was as mad as _____.

6. Of course I've heard that joke before! It's as old as _____.

7. Nicole felt very embarrassed. She turned as red as _____.

8. I tend to be a little messy, but my roommate is as neat as _____.

9. When Erica received the good news, she felt as high as _____.

10. How can anyone expect me to sleep in this bed? It's as hard as _____.

13-2 COMPARATIVE AND SUPERLATIVE

(a) "A" is *older than* "B." (b) "A" and "B" are *older than* "C" and "D." (c) Ed is *more generous than* his brother.	The comparative compares "this/these" to "that/those." Form: *-er* or *more*. (See Chart 13-3.) NOTICE: A comparative is followed by *than*.
(d) "A", "B", "C", and "D" are sisters. "A" is *the oldest* of all four sisters. (e) A woman in Turkey claims to be *the oldest person* in the world. (f) Ed is *the most generous person* in his family.	The superlative compares one part of a whole group to all the rest of the group. Form: *-est* or *most*. (See Chart 13-3 for forms.) NOTICE: A superlative begins with *the*.

□ **EXERCISE 6—ERROR ANALYSIS:** All of the following sentences contain errors. Find and correct the mistakes.

1. Alaska is large than Texas.

   → *Alaska is larger than Texas.*

2. Alaska is largest state in the United States.

3. Texas is the larger from France in land area.

4. Old shoes are usually more comfortable that new shoes.

5. My running shoes are the more comfortable shoes I own.

6. My running shoes are more comfortable as my boots.

7. Mr. Molina writes the most clearly than Ms. York.

8. English is the most widely used language from the world.

9. I have one sister and one brother. My sister is younger in the family.

10. Mark's knife was as sharper from a razor blade.

11. I like Chinese food more better than French food.

13-3 COMPARATIVE AND SUPERLATIVE FORMS OF ADJECTIVES AND ADVERBS

		COMPARATIVE	SUPERLATIVE	
ONE-SYLLABLE ADJECTIVES	old wise	older wiser	the oldest the wisest	For most one-syllable adjectives, **-er** and **-est** are added.
TWO-SYLLABLE ADJECTIVES	famous pleasant	more famous more pleasant	the most famous the most pleasant	For most two-syllable adjectives, **more** and **most** are used.
	busy pretty	busier prettier	the busiest the prettiest	**-Er/-est** are used with two-syllable adjectives that end in -y. The -y is changed to -i.
	clever gentle friendly	cleverer more clever gentler more gentle friendlier more friendly	the cleverest the most clever the gentlest the most gentle the friendliest the most friendly	Some two-syllable adjectives use **-er/-est** or **more/most**: able, angry, clever, common, cruel, friendly, gentle, handsome, narrow, pleasant, polite, quiet, simple, sour.
ADJECTIVES WITH THREE OR MORE SYLLABLES	important fascinating	more important more fascinating	the most important the most fascinating	**More** and **most** are used with long adjectives.
IRREGULAR ADJECTIVES	good bad	better worse	the best the worst	**Good** and **bad** have irregular comparative and superlative forms.
-LY ADVERBS	carefully slowly	more carefully more slowly	the most carefully the most slowly	**More** and **most** are used with adverbs that end in **-ly**.*
ONE-SYLLABLE ADVERBS	fast hard	faster harder	the fastest the hardest	The **-er** and **-est** forms are used with one-syllable adverbs.
IRREGULAR ADVERBS	well badly far	better worse farther/further**	the best the worst the farthest/furthest	

*Exception: **early** is both an adjective and an adverb. Forms: *earlier, earliest.*

Both **farther and **further** are used to compare physical distances: *I walked farther/further than my friend did.* **Further** (but not **farther**) can also mean "additional": *I need further information.*

☐ **EXERCISE 7:** Give the COMPARATIVE and SUPERLATIVE forms of the following adjectives and adverbs.

1. high → **higher, the highest**
2. careful
3. slow
4. slowly
5. active
6. funny
7. wet⋆
8. sweet⋆
9. late⋆
10. thin
11. clean
12. serious

13. good
14. bad
15. clear
16. clearly
17. happy
18. confusing
19. courageous
20. common
21. friendly
22. red
23. wild
24. dangerous

☐ **EXERCISE 8—ORAL:** Choose five to ten movable objects (in this room or in the possession of anyone in this room) and put them in a central place. Compare the items using the given words. Use both the COMPARATIVE (*-er/more*) and the SUPERLATIVE (*-est/most*).

Example: big/small
STUDENT A: Omar's pen is bigger than Anya's ring.
STUDENT B: Sergio's calculator is smaller than Kim's briefcase.
STUDENT C: The biggest thing on the table is the briefcase.
STUDENT D: Etc.

1. big/small
2. soft/hard
3. rough/smooth
4. light/heavy

5. cheap/expensive
6. new/old
7. important/unimportant
8. common/unusual

⋆Spelling notes:
- When a one-syllable adjective ends in **one vowel + a consonant**, double the consonant and add *-er/-est*. Example: *hot, hotter, hottest.*
- When an adjective ends in **two vowels + a consonant**, do NOT double the consonant: *cool, cooler, coolest.*
- When an adjective ends in *-e*, do NOT double the consonant: ***wide, wider, widest.***

13-4 USING COMPARATIVES

(a) I'm older *than **my brother*** (*is*). (b) I'm older *than **he** is*. (c) I'm older *than **him***. (*informal*)	In formal English, a subject pronoun (e.g., *he*) follows ***than***, as in (b). In everday, informal spoken English, an object pronoun (e.g., *him*) often follows ***than***, as in (c).
(d) He works harder *than **I do***. (e) I arrived earlier *than **they did***.	Frequently an auxiliary verb follows the subject after ***than***. In (d): *than I do = than I work*.
(f) Tom is ***much/a lot/far** older* than I am. INCORRECT: Tom is very older than I am. (g) Ann drives ***much/a lot/far** more carefully* than she used to. (h) Ben is ***a little** (**bit**) older* than me.	***Very*** often modifies adjectives and adverbs: e.g., *Tom is very old. He drives very carefully.* However, ***very*** is NOT used to modify comparative adjectives and adverbs. Instead, they are often modified by ***much**, **a lot**,* or ***far***, as in (f) and (g). Another common modifier is ***a little/a little bit***, as in (h).
(i) A pen is ***less** expensive **than*** a book. (j) A pen is ***not as** expensive **as*** a book. (k) A pen is *not as large as* a book. INCORRECT: A pen is less large than a book.	The opposite of ***-er/more*** is expressed by ***less*** or ***not as . . . as***. (i) and (j) have the same meaning. ***Less** (**not as . . . as***) is used with adjectives and adverbs of **more than one syllable**. Only ***not as . . . as*** (NOT *less*) is used with one-syllable adjectives or adverbs, as in (k).

☐ **EXERCISE 9:** Complete the following. Use pronouns in the completions.

1. My sister is only six. She's much younger than _____ **I am** _____
    OR: *(informally)* **me** _____.

2. Peggy is thirteen, and she feels sad. She thinks most of the other girls in school are far more popular than _____.

3. The children can't lift that heavy box, but Mr. Ford can. He's stronger than _____.

4. Jim isn't a very good typist. I can type much faster than _____.

5. I was on time. Jack was late. I got there earlier than _____.

6. Ted is out of shape. I can run a lot faster and farther than _____.

☐ **EXERCISE 10—ORAL:** Add *very, **much**, a lot,* or *far* to the following sentences.

1. It's hot today. → *It's **very** hot today.*
2. It's hotter today than yesterday. → *It's **much/a lot/far** hotter today . . . .*
3. Learning a second language is difficult.
4. Learning a second language is more difficult than learning chemistry formulas.
5. An airplane is fast.
6. Taking an airplane is faster than hitchhiking.
7. You can live more inexpensively in student housing than in a rented apartment.
8. You can live inexpensively in student housing.

☐ **EXERCISE 11—ORAL:** All of the following sentences contain *not as . . . as.* If possible, change them to sentences with the same meaning using *less.*

1. I don't live as close to my brother as I do to my sister.
   → (*no change using **less***)
2. I don't visit my brother as often as I visit my sister.
   → *I visit my brother less often than I visit my sister.*
3. George isn't as nice as his brother.
4. George isn't as generous as his brother.
5. I'm not as eager to go to the circus as the children are.
6. A notebook isn't as expensive as a textbook.
7. Wood isn't as hard as metal.
8. Some people think that life in a city isn't as peaceful as life in a small town.
9. The moon isn't nearly as far from the earth as the sun is.
10. I don't travel to Europe on business as frequently as I used to.

☐ **EXERCISE 12:** Complete the following with comparatives by using *more/-er* or *less,* as appropriate. Use the words in parentheses plus your own words.

1. This test wasn't hard. It was a lot (*difficult*) **less difficult than the last test.**

2. Dr. Lee's tests are far (*difficult*) **more difficult than Dr. Barton's tests.**

3. A piano is a lot (*heavy*) _____

4. To me, science is much (*interesting*) _____

5. Saltwater is (*dense*) _____

6. People are far (*intelligent*) _____

7. Fish are considerably (*intelligent*) _____

8. She rarely comes to see us. She visits us much (*frequently*) _____

9. When you're hot and tired, nothing is (*refreshing*) _____

10. In my life, I have always tried to help those who are (*fortunate*) _____

☐ **EXERCISE 13—ORAL (BOOKS CLOSED):** Answer the question. Begin your response with "Not really, but at least...."

"Not really, but at least . . ." (*Written on the board.*)

Example: Is the mayor of this city famous?
Response: Not really, but at least s/he is more famous than I am.

1. Is the weather warm/cold today?
2. Is a mouse big?
3. Is this room large?
4. Is your desk comfortable?
5. Is an elephant intelligent?
6. Was the last exercise easy?
7. Is the floor clean?
8. Is a pen expensive?
9. Is this book heavy?
10. Are you relaxed right now?
11. Is blue a bright color?
12. Is (*name of a city*) close to (*name of this city*)?

13-5 USING *MORE* WITH NOUNS

(a) Would you like some **more coffee**? (b) Not everyone is here. I expect **more people** to come later.	In (a): "coffee" is a noun. When **more** is used with nouns, it often has the meaning of *additional*. It is not necessary to use **than**.
(c) There are **more people** in China **than** there are in the United States.	**More** is also used with nouns to make complete comparisons by using **than**.
(d) Do you have enough coffee, or would you like some **more**?	When the meaning is clear, the noun may be omitted and **more** used by itself.

☐ **EXERCISE 14:** Use *-er* or **more** and the words in the list to complete the following. Discuss whether the words are nouns, adjectives, or adverbs and review how comparatives are formed with each of these parts of speech. When do you use *-er* and when do you use **more**?

✔bright	happiness	people	responsibly
✔brightly	happy	quick	salt
doctors	information	responsibilities	✔traffic
happily	mistakes	responsible	

1. A city has _____**more traffic**_____ than a small town.

2. Sunlight is much _____**brighter**_____ than moonlight.

3. Did you know that a laser burns billions of times **_more brightly_** than the light at the sun's surface?

4. There is _____ about geography in an encyclopedia than (there is) in a dictionary.

5. I used to be sad, but now I'm a lot _____ about my life (than I used to be).

6. Unhappy roommates or spouses can live together _____ _____ if they learn to respect each other's differences.

7. She's had a miserable life. I hope she finds _____ in the future.

8. I made _____ on the last test than (I did) on the first one, so I got a worse grade.

9. My daughter Annie is trustworthy and mature. She behaves much _____ than my nephew Louie.

10. A twelve-year-old has _____ at home and in school than a nine-year-old.

11. My son is _____ about doing his homework than his older sister is.

12. A rabbit is _____ than a turtle.

13. This soup doesn't taste quite right. I think it needs just a little

    _____.

14. Health care in rural areas is poor. We need _____ to treat people in rural areas.

15. At present, approximately two-fifths of the world's population can speak English. English is taught to _____ in the world than any other language is or ever has been.

13-6 REPEATING A COMPARATIVE

(a) Because he was afraid, he walked **_faster and faster_**.	Repeating a comparative gives the idea that something becomes progressively greater, i.e., it increases in intensity, quality, or quantity.
(b) Life in the modern world is becoming **_more and more complex_**.	

□ **EXERCISE 15:** Using the words in the following list or your own words, complete the sentences. Repeat the comparative.

angry	*enthusiastic*	*long*
big	*good*	*loud*
discouraged	*hot*	

1. Her English is improving. It is getting _____ **better and better** _____.

2. They just had their sixth child. Their family is getting _____.

3. The line of people waiting to get into the theater got _____.

4. As the soccer game progressed, the crowd became _____.

5. The weather is getting _____ with each passing day.

6. I've been looking for a job for a month and still haven't been able to find one. I'm getting _____.

7. As the ambulance came closer to us, the siren became _____.

8. She sat there quietly, but during all that time she was getting _____. Finally she exploded.

13-7 USING DOUBLE COMPARATIVES

(a) **The harder** you study, **the more** you will learn.	A double comparative has two parts; both parts begin with *the*, as in the examples. The second part of the comparison is the **result** of the first part.
(b) **The older** he got, **the quieter** he became.	
(c) **The more** she studied, **the more** she learned.	
(d) **The warmer** the weather (is), **the better** I like it.	In (a): If you study harder, the result will be that you will learn more.
(e) A: Should we ask Jenny and Jim to the party too? B: Why not? **The more, the merrier**.	**The more, the merrier** and **the sooner, the better** are two common expressions. In (e): It is good to have more people at the party.
(f) A: When should we leave? B: **The sooner, the better**.	In (f): It is good if we leave as soon as we can.

☐ **EXERCISE 16:** Combine the ideas in the parentheses into a DOUBLE COMPARATIVE. You need to decide which of the two given ideas should come first in the comparison to make a logical statement.

1. (*I became bored. He talked.*)
   I met a man at a party last night. I tried to be interested in what he was saying, but the . . . *more he talked, the more bored I became.*

2. (*I waited long. I got angry.*)
   My friend told me that she would pick me up at the corner at seven o'clock. By seven-thirty, she still hadn't come. The . . . .

3. (*You understand more. You are old.*)
   There are many advantages to being young, but the . . . .

4. (*She drove fast. I became nervous.*)
   Erica offered to take me to the airport, and I was grateful. But we got a late start, so on the way she stepped on the accelerator. I got more than a little uncomfortable. The . . . .

5. (*He thought about his family. He became homesick.*)
   Pierre tried to concentrate on his studying, but his mind would drift to his family and his home. The . . . .

6. (*We ran fast to reach the house. The sky grew dark.*)
   A storm was threatening. The . . . .

7. (*I became confused. I thought about it.*)
   At first I thought I'd understood what she'd said, but then the . . . .

8. (*The air is polluted. The chances of developing respiratory diseases are great.*)
   Pollution poses many dangers. For example, the . . . .

13-8 USING SUPERLATIVES

(a) Tokyo is one of **the largest cities in the world**.	Typical completions when a superlative is used:
(b) David is **the most generous person I have ever known**.	In (a): superlative + *in* a place (*the world, this class, my family, the corporation*, etc.)
(c) I have three books. These two are quite good, but this one is the **best** (book) **of all**.	In (b): superlative + adjective clause. In (c): superlative + *of all*.
(d) I took four final exams. The final in accounting was **the least difficult** of all.	*The least* has the opposite meaning of *the most*.

☐ **EXERCISE 17:** Use the appropriate SUPERLATIVE form (*most* or *-est*) for the word in parentheses and complete the sentences with your own words.

1. Physics is (*difficult*) __the most difficult__ course __I have ever taken__ .

2. My grandparents are (*wise*) _____ people

   _____ .

3. My hometown is (*friendly*) _____ place

   _____ .

4. What is (*embarrassing*) _____ experience

   _____ ?

5. Who is (*important*) _____ political figure

   _____ ?

6. What is (*high*) _____ mountain _____ ?

7. Margaret is one of (*lazy*) _____ people _____ .

*Use **least** in the following:*

8. Ed is not lazy, but he is certainly one of (*ambitious*) _____

   people _____ .

9. I always look for (*expensive*) _____ items _____ .

10. What is (*useful*) _____ or (*important*) _____

    _____ thing _____ ?

☐ **EXERCISE 18:** Use SUPERLATIVES of the given words and your own words to complete the sentences.

1. *bad*   __"Sea Monsters"__ is the _____ __worst__ _____ movie

   __I've ever seen__ .

2. *popular*   The _____ sport in _____ is

   _____ .

3. *large*   The _____ city in _____ is

   _____ .

4. *good*   _____ is the _____

   restaurant in _____ .

5. *good*   One of the _____ places to eat in

   _____ is _____ .

6. *famous*   _____ is one of the _____

people in _____.

7. *hot*   There are several hot months, but _____ is

usually the _____ of all.

8. *valuable*   The _____ thing I have is _____.

9. *important*   The three _____ things in life are _____

_____.

10. *serious*   The _____ problems in _____

today are _____.

☐ **EXERCISE 19—ORAL:** Compare the items in each list using the given words. Use *as ...as*, the COMPARATIVE (*-er/more*), and the SUPERLATIVE (*-est/most*).

　　Example:　roads in this city: *wide/narrow/busy/dangerous*
　　Responses:　First Avenue is *wider* than Market Street.
　　　　　　　Second Avenue is *nearly as wide as* First Avenue.
　　　　　　　First Avenue is *narrower* than Interstate Highway 70.
　　　　　　　Highway 70 is *the widest* of all the roads in this city.
　　　　　　　It is also *the busiest.*
　　　　　　　Usually First Avenue is *busier* than Market Street.
　　　　　　　The most dangerous street in the city is Olive Boulevard.
　　　　　　　Etc.

1. a lemon, a grapefruit, and an orange:
　　sweet/sour/large/small
2. this book, that book, and that book:
　　thin/fat/interesting/useful/good/bad
3. a kitten, a cheetah, and a lion:
　　weak/powerful/wild/gentle/fast
4. air, water, and wood:
　　heavy/light/important to human life
5. boxing, soccer, and golf:
　　dangerous/safe/exciting/boring
6. three movies you have seen:
　　good/bad/exciting/sad
7. the food (at places in this city where you have eaten):
　　delicious/appetizing/inexpensive/good/bad
8. sounds or noises:
　　loud/soft/pleasant/annoying
9. geographical regions:
　　mountainous/flat/dry/humid/populated/unpopulated

13-9 USING *THE SAME, SIMILAR, DIFFERENT, LIKE, ALIKE*

(a) John and Mary have *the same books*. (b) John and Mary have *similar books*. (c) John and Mary have *different books*. (d) Their books are *the same*. (e) Their books are *similar*. (f) Their books are *different*.	*The same*, *similar*, and *different* are used as adjectives. Notice: *the* always precedes *same*.
(g) This book is *the same as* that one. (h) This book is *similar to* that one. (i) This book is *different from* that one.	Notice: *the same* is followed by *as*; *similar* is followed by *to*; *different* is followed by *from*.★
(j) She is *the same age as* my mother. My shoes are *the same size as* yours.	A noun may come between *the same* and *as*, as in (j).
(k) My pen *is like* your pen. (l) My pen and your pen *are alike*.	Notice in (k) and (l): *noun* + *be like* + *noun* *noun* and *noun* + *be alike*
(m) She *looks like* her sister. It *looks like* rain. It *sounds like* thunder. This material *feels like* silk. That *smells like* gas. This chemical *tastes like* salt. Stop *acting like* a fool. He *seems like* a nice fellow.	In addition to following *be*, *like* also follows certain verbs, primarily those dealing with the senses. Notice the examples in (m).
(n) The twins *look alike*. We *think alike*. Most four-year-olds *act alike*. My sister and I *talk alike*. The little boys *are dressed alike*.	*Alike* may follow a few verbs other than *be*. Notice the examples in (n).

★In informal speech, native speakers might use *than* instead of *from* after *different*. *From* is considered correct in formal English, unless the comparison is completed by a clause: *I have a different attitude now than I used to have.*

☐ **EXERCISE 20:** Use *the same (as), similar (to), different (from), like,* and *alike* in the following. There may be more than one possible response in some of the sentences. Use whatever response sounds best to you.

1. Jennifer and Jack both come from Rapid City. In other words, they come from _____*the same*_____ town.

2. This city is _____*the same as/similar to/like*_____ my hometown. Both are quiet and conservative.

3. You and I don't agree. Your ideas are _____ mine.

4. Eric never wears _____ clothes two days in a row.

5. Ants are fascinating. An ant colony is _____ a well-disciplined army.

6. In terms of shape, cabbage looks _____ lettuce. But cabbage and lettuce don't taste _____.

7. A male mosquito is not _____ size _____ a female mosquito. The female is larger.

8. I'm used to strong coffee. I think the coffee most North Americans drink tastes _____ dishwater!

9. The pronunciation of "caught" is _____ the pronunciation of "cot."

10. "Meet" and "meat" are homonyms; i.e., they have _____ pronunciation.

11. My dictionary is _____ yours.

12. Trying to get through school without studying is _____ trying to go swimming without getting wet.

13. "Flower" has _____ pronunciation _____ "flour."

14. A crocodile and an alligator are _____ in appearance.

15. If it looks _____ a duck, quacks _____ a duck, and walks _____ a duck, it is a duck. (*a humorous saying*)

☐ **EXERCISE 21—ORAL:** Do you have sayings in your language that are similar to or the same as the following English proverbs?

1. Don't count your chickens before they hatch.
2. The early bird gets the worm.
3. Too many cooks spoil the broth.
4. A bird in the hand is worth two in the bush.
5. A stitch in time saves nine.
6. When in Rome, do as the Romans do.
7. Birds of a feather flock together.
8. A rolling stone gathers no moss.

☐ **EXERCISE 22—ORAL:** Before you come to class, prepare statements of comparison and contrast on the following topics. Be inventive, original, and specific. Prepare at least three statements on each topic to share with the rest of the class.

Topics:

1. Language
2. Food
3. Seasons of the year
4. Children/adults
5. Sports

☐ **EXERCISE 23—WRITTEN:** Following are topics for writing.

Compare and contrast:

1. Being single and being married.
2. Cities you have lived in or have visited.
3. Different schools you have attended.
4. Your way of life before and after you became a parent.
5. Yourself now to yourself ten years ago.
6. Your country now to your country 100 years ago.
7. Life today to life 100 years from now.

CHAPTER *14*

Noun Clauses

14-1 NOUN CLAUSES: INTRODUCTION

(a) $\overset{S}{I}$ $\overset{V}{know}$ $\overset{O}{his\ address.}$ (noun phrase)	Verbs are often followed by objects. The object is usually a noun phrase,* as in (a): **his address** is a noun phrase; **his address** is the object of the verb *know*.
(b) $\overset{S}{I}$ $\overset{V}{know}$ $\overset{O}{where\ he\ lives.}$ (noun clause)	Some verbs can be followed by noun clauses.* In (b): **where he lives** is a noun clause; **where he lives** is the object of the verb *know*.
$\overset{S}{}$ $\overset{V}{}$ $\overset{O}{\overset{S\quad V}{}}$ (c) I know **where he lives.**	A noun clause has its own subject and verb. In (c): **he** is the subject of the noun clause; **lives** is the verb of the noun clause.
(d) I know **where he lives.** (noun clause)	A noun clause can begin with a question word. (See 14-2.)
(e) I don't know **if he is married.** (noun clause)	A noun clause can begin with **if** or **whether**. (See 14-4.)
(f) I know **that the world is round.** (noun clause)	A noun clause can begin with **that**. (See 14-5.)

*Grammar terminology:

A **phrase** is a group of related words. It does not contain a subject and a verb.

A **clause** is a group of related words. It contains a subject and a verb.

A noun clause is a dependent clause and cannot stand alone as a sentence. It must be connected to an independent clause (a main clause).

14-2 NOUN CLAUSES THAT BEGIN WITH A QUESTION WORD

The following question words can be used to introduce a noun clause: *when*, *where*, *why*, *how*, *who*, *whom*, *what*, *which*, *whose*.

INFORMATION QUESTIONS	NOUN CLAUSES	Notice in the examples: Question word order is NOT used in a noun clause.
Where *does he live*?	(a) I don't know *where he lives*.	INCORRECT: *I know where does he live.* CORRECT: *I know where he lives.*
When *did they leave*?	(b) Do you know *when they left*?	
What *did she say*?	(c) Please tell me *what she said*.	
Why *is Tom* absent?	(d) I wonder *why Tom is* absent.	

□ **EXERCISE 1:** Complete the sentences by changing the questions to noun clauses.

1. *Where did Paul go?* I don't know _____ **where Paul went.** _____

2. *How old is Kate?* I don't know _____

3. *Why did Tim leave?* I don't know _____

4. *When did Tim leave?* I don't know _____

5. *Where did he go?* I don't know _____

6. *Where is he?* I don't know _____

7. *Where does he live?* I don't remember _____

8. *What did he say?* I didn't hear _____

9. *Where is the post office?* Could you please tell me _____

10. *What time is it?* Could you please tell me _____

11. *How much does this book cost?* Could you please tell me _____

12. *What does this word mean?* Could you please tell me _____

13. *What country is Anna from?* Do you know _____

14. *Why was Kathy absent yesterday?* Do you know _____

15. *How far is it to Chicago?* I wonder _____

16. *When does the semester end?* Can you tell me _____

17. *What is Sue talking about?* I don't understand _____

18. *When did David arrive?* I don't know _____

19. *When is he going to leave?* Do you know _____

20. *Where can I buy a good radio?* Do you know _____

□ **EXERCISE 2:** Complete the sentences by changing the questions to noun clauses.

1. *Who(m) did you see at the party?* Tell me **who(m) you saw at the party.**

2. *Who came to the party?* Tell me _____ **who came to the party.★** _____

3. *Who(m) did Helen talk to?* Do you know _____

4. *Who lives in that apartment?* Do you know _____ _____

5. *What happened?* Tell me _____

6. *What did he say?* Tell me _____

7. *What kind of car does Pat have?* I can't remember _____

8. *How old are their children?* I can't ever remember _____

9. *Why did you say that?* I don't understand _____

10. *Where can I catch the bus?* Could you please tell me _____

11. *Who broke the window?* Do you know _____

12. *Who did Sara invite?* I don't know _____

13. *How long has Ted been living here?* Do you know _____

14. *What time is flight 677 supposed to arrive?*

    Can you tell me _____

15. *Why is Yoko angry?* Do you know _____

14-3 NOUN CLAUSES WITH *WHO, WHAT, WHOSE + BE*

QUESTION	NOUN CLAUSE	
V S Who ⌐is⌐ *that boy*?	(a) I don't know who ⌐*that boy*⌐*is*.	A noun or pronoun that follows main verb *be* in a question comes in front of *be* in a noun clause, as in (a) and (b). A prepositional phrase (e.g., *in the office*) does NOT come in front of *be* in a noun clause, as in (c) and (d).
V S Whose pen ⌐is⌐ *this*?	(b) I don't know whose pen ⌐*this*⌐*is*.	
S V ⌐*Who*⌐*is*⌐ in the office?	(c) I don't know ⌐*who*⌐*is*⌐ in the office.	
S V ⌐*Whose pen*⌐*is*⌐ on the desk?	(d) I don't know ⌐*whose pen*⌐*is*⌐ on the desk.	

★Usual question word order is not used when the question word (e.g., *who* or *what*) is the subject of a question. (See Charts 6-2 and 6-3.) In this case, the word order in the noun clause is the same as the word order in the question.

□ **EXERCISE 3:** Complete the sentences by changing the questions to noun clauses.

1. *Who is she?* I don't know _____

2. *Who are they?* I don't know _____

3. *What is that?* Do you know _____

4. *What are those?* Can you tell me _____

5. *Whose book is that?* I don't know _____

6. *Whose books are those?* Do you know _____

7. *What is a wrench?* Do you know _____

8. *Who is that woman?* I wonder _____

9. *Whose house is that?* I wonder _____

10. *What is a clause?* Don't you know _____

11. *What is in that drawer?* I don't know _____

12. *Who is in that room?* I don't know _____

13. *Whose car is in the driveway?* Do you know _____

14. *Whose car is that?* Do you know _____

15. *What is on TV tonight?* I wonder _____

16. *What is a carrot?* Do you know _____

17. *Whose glasses are those?* Could you tell me _____

18. *Who am I?* He doesn't know _____

19. *What's at the end of the rainbow?* The little girl wants to know _____
_____

☐ **EXERCISE 4—ORAL (BOOKS CLOSED):** Change the questions to noun clauses. Begin your response with "*I don't know* . . . ."

> *Example:* Where does (. . .) live?
> *Response:* I don't know where (. . .) lives.

1. Where did (. . .) go yesterday?
2. What did (. . .) buy yesterday?
3. Why is (. . .) absent?
4. Where is (. . .)?
5. How old is (. . .)?
6. Where does (. . .) live?
7. Where does (. . .) eat lunch?
8. What is (. . .)'s last name?
9. Why does (. . .) go downtown every day?
10. What time does (. . .) usually get up?
11. Why did (. . .) go downtown yesterday?
12. When did (. . .) get home last night?
13. What time did (. . .) go to bed last night?
14. What time is it?
15. What time does (. . .) eat dinner?
16. How long has (. . .) been living here?
17. Who broke that window?
18. Who did (. . .) call last night?
19. What happened in (Brazil) yesterday?
20. What did (. . .) eat for breakfast?
21. Who wrote (*War and Peace*)?
22. Who did (. . .) see yesterday?
23. What caused the earthquake in (Iran)?
24. What causes earthquakes?
25. Who is that girl?
26. Who are those people?
27. Whose (backpack) is that?
28. Whose (gloves) are those?
29. What kind of tree is that?
30. What kind of car does (. . .) have?

☐ **EXERCISE 5—ORAL (BOOKS CLOSED):** STUDENT A: Change the noun clause to a question. STUDENT B: Answer the question.

> *Example:* Ask (. . .) where (. . .) lives.
> TEACHER TO A: Toshi, ask Ingrid where Mustafa lives.
> STUDENT A: Ingrid, where does Mustafa live?
> STUDENT B: I don't know where Mustafa lives. OR: Mustafa lives in Reed Hall.

1. Ask (. . .) where (. . .) ate breakfast this morning.
2. Ask (. . .) what (. . .)'s favorite color is.
3. Ask (. . .) when (. . .) got up this morning.
4. Ask (. . .) why (. . .) isn't sitting in his/her usual seat today.
5. Ask (. . .) how (. . .) got to class today.
6. Ask (. . .) who (. . .) lives with.
7. Offer (. . .) this (*candy bar*) and that (*candy bar*). Ask him/her which one he/she wants.
8. Ask (. . .) what time it is.
9. Ask (. . .) what kind of watch (. . .) has.

10. Ask (. . .) why (. . .) didn't come to class yesterday.
11. Ask (. . .) who (. . .)'s best friend is.
12. Ask (. . .) where (. . .) went after class yesterday.

☐ **EXERCISE 6—ORAL (BOOKS CLOSED):** Change the questions to noun clauses. Begin your response with "*Could you please tell me . . . .*"

Example: Where does (. . .) live?
Response: Could you please tell me where (. . .) lives?

1. What time is it?
2. Where is the post office?
3. Where is the library?
4. Where is the rest room?
5. How much does this pen cost?
6. How much does this book cost?
7. How much do these shoes cost?
8. What does this word mean?
9. What does "complex" mean?
10. What does "steam" mean?
11. Where is the nearest hospital?
12. Why were you late for class?
13. Where can I buy a garden hose?
14. What is a garden hose?
15. Whose pen is this?
16. Whose papers are those?

☐ **EXERCISE 7—ORAL (BOOKS CLOSED):** Practice using noun clauses while reviewing irregular verbs. Begin your response with "*I don't know . . . .*"

Example: What did (. . .) find?
Response: I don't know what he/she found.

1. Where did (. . .) sit yesterday?
2. What did (. . .) wear yesterday?
3. When did (. . .) wake up?
4. What did (. . .) buy?
5. Where did (. . .) lose his/her umbrella?
6. How did (. . .) tear his shirt/her blouse?
7. Who did (. . .) speak to yesterday?
8. How long did (. . .) sleep last night?
9. What did (. . .) make for dinner last night?
10. What did (. . .) give (. . .) for his/her birthday?
11. Why did (. . .) fly to New York?
12. What did (. . .) steal?
13. How much money did (. . .) lend (. . .)?
14. Why did (. . .) fall down?
15. Which book did (. . .) choose?
16. When did (. . .) quit smoking?
17. What did (. . .) see?
18. Why did (. . .) shake his/her head?
19. Why did (. . .) bring his/her radio to class?
20. Why did (. . .) take your dictionary?
21. Why did (. . .) draw a picture?
22. Who did (. . .) write a letter to?
23. How did (. . .) meet his wife/her husband?

24. Why did (. . .) bite his/her lip?
25. When did this (*term, session, semester*) begin?
26. How did (. . .) break his/her arm?
27. How did (. . .) catch a cold?
28. When did (. . .) get married?
29. When did (. . .) do his/her homework?
30. Where did (. . .) grow up?

14-4 NOUN CLAUSES WHICH BEGIN WITH *IF* OR *WHETHER★*

YES/NO QUESTION	NOUN CLAUSE	
Is Eric at home? Does the bus stop here? Did Alice go to Chicago?	S — V — O (a) I don't know *if Eric is at home*. (b) Do you know *if the bus stops here*? (c) I wonder *if Alice went to Chicago*.	When a yes/no question is changed to a noun clause, *if* is usually used to introduce the clause.
(d) I don't know *if Eric is at home or not*.	When *if* introduces a noun clause, the expression *or not* may come at the end of the clause, as in (d).	
(e) I don't know *whether Eric is at home*. (f) I don't know *whether Eric is at home or not*. (g) I don't know *whether or not Eric is at home*.	In (e): *whether* has the same meaning as *if*. In (f): *or not* can come at the end of the noun clause. In (g): *or not* can come immediately after *whether*. (NOTE: *or not* cannot come immediately after *if*.)	

★See Chart 15-5 for the use of *if* and *whether* with *ask* in reported speech.

☐ **EXERCISE 8—ORAL:** Complete the sentences by changing the yes/no questions to noun clauses. Introduce the noun clause with *if* or *whether*. Practice using *or not*.

1. *Is Mary at the library?* I don't know . . . .
   → . . . *if Mary is at the library*.
   . . . *if Mary is at the library or not*.
   . . . *whether Mary is at the library*.
   . . . *whether Mary is at the library or not*.
   . . . *whether or not Mary is at the library*.

2. *Does Bob live in an apartment?* I don't know . . . .

3. *Did Joe go downtown?* I don't know . . . .

4. *Will Ann be in class tomorrow?* I wonder . . . .

5. *Is Tom at home?* Do you know . . . .

☐ **EXERCISE 9:** Change the questions to noun clauses.

1. *Did Steve go to the bank?* I don't know ____*if (whether) Steve went*____
   ____*to the bank.*____

2. *Where did Steve go?* I don't know ____*where Steve went.*____

3. *Is Karen at home?* Do you know _____

4. *Where is Karen?* Do you know _____

5. *How is Pat feeling today?* I wonder _____

6. *Is Pat feeling better today?* I wonder _____

7. *Does the bus stop here?* Do you know _____

8. *Where does the bus stop?* I wonder _____

9. *Why is Elena absent today?*

   The teacher wants to know _____

10. *Is Elena going to be absent again tomorrow?*

    I wonder _____

11. *Where did Janet go last night?* Do you know _____

12. *Should I buy that book?* I wonder _____

13. *Which book should I buy?* I wonder _____

14. *Can Jerry speak French?* I don't know _____

15. *How much does that book cost?* Do you know _____

16. *Is there life on other planets?* No one knows _____

17. *Are we going to have a test tomorrow?*

    Let's ask the teacher _____

18. *Is there a Santa Claus?*

    The little boy wants to know _____

19. *Who is that man?* I'm going to ask Nicole _____

20. *Is that man a teacher?* I'm going to ask Nicole _____

☐ **EXERCISE 10—ORAL (BOOKS CLOSED):** Make sentences with noun clauses. Begin your response with "*I wonder ....*"

        Example: Did (...) go to the bank?
        Response: I wonder if (...) went to the bank.

        Example: Where did (...) go?
        Response: I wonder where (...) went.

1. Why is (...) absent today?
2. Where is (...)?
3. Is (...) sick?
4. Will it (snow) tomorrow?
5. Will the weather be nice tomorrow?
6. Is (...) going to be in class tomorrow?
7. How long has (...) been living here?
8. Did (...) go to the library last night?
9. How much does (a Rolls Royce) cost?
10. Where did (...) go last night?
11. Who lives in that house?
12. Who is that woman?
13. Is that woman a teacher?
14. Whose (book) is that?
15. Whose (gloves) are those?
16. Whose (pen) is that?
17. Whose (papers) are those?
18. Did (...) study last night?
19. Does (...) have a car?
20. How far is it to (St. Louis)?

☐ **EXERCISE 11:** Change the questions to noun clauses.

1. *Will it rain tomorrow?* I wonder ___***if it will rain tomorrow.***___

2. *What is an amphibian?*

   Do you know _____

3. *Is a frog an amphibian?*

   Can you tell me _____

4. *What's on TV tonight?*

   I wonder _____

5. *What is the speed of sound?*

   Do you know _____

6. *Does sound travel faster than light?*

   Do you know _____

7. *Are dogs color blind?*

   Do you know _____

8. *Why is the sky blue?*

   Annie wants to know _____

9. *Does that store accept credit cards?*

   Do you know _____

10. *Do insects have ears?*

    The little girl wants to know _____

11. *When will the next earthquake occur in California?*

    No one knows _____

12. *Will there be another earthquake in California this year?*

    No one knows _____

13. *Do animals have the same emotions as human beings?*

    The little boy wants to know _____

14. *How do dolphins communicate with each other?*

    Do scientists know _____

15. *Can people communicate with dolphins?*

    I want to find out _____

16. *Have beings from outer space ever visited the earth?*

    I wonder _____

☐ **EXERCISE 12—ORAL (BOOKS CLOSED):** Make sentences with noun clauses.

> STUDENT A: Ask a question beginning with "*Do you know . . . ?*"
> STUDENT B: Answer "*no.*" Give a short answer and then a full answer.
>
> *Example:* Does (. . .) live in the dorm?
> STUDENT A: Do you know if (. . .) lives in the dorm?
> STUDENT B: No, I don't. I don't know whether or not (. . .) lives in the dorm.
>
> *Example:* Where does (. . .) live?
> STUDENT A: Do you know where (. . .) lives?
> STUDENT B: No, I don't. I don't know where (. . .) lives.

1. Does (. . .) have (a car)?
2. Who is (that woman)?
3. Can (. . .) sing?
4. What does "gossip" mean?
5. What time does the mail come?
6. Is the mail here yet?
7. Does (. . .) have a job?
8. Is (. . .) married?
9. Why is (. . .) absent today?
10. Is (the library) open on Sundays?
11. What time does (the bookstore) close?
12. Does (. . .) speak (*language*)?
13. What kind of (car) does (. . .) have?
14. Is (. . .) planning to take another English course?
15. Is there a pay phone in this building?

☐ **EXERCISE 13—ORAL:** Answer the questions using the given words.

> QUESTION 1: What do you know?
>   a. *where*
>   → STUDENT A: I know *where* Madagascar is located.
>   STUDENT B: I know *where* (. . .)'s dictionary is.
>   STUDENT C: I know *where* my parents got married.
>   STUDENT D: I know *where* the Blueberry Cafe is.
>   STUDENT E: etc.
>   b. *what*
>   c. *why*
>   d. *who*

QUESTION 2:   What do you NOT know?
   a. *where*
      → STUDENT A: I don't know *where* Madagascar is located.
         STUDENT B: etc.
   b. *if*
   c. *why*
   d. *who*

QUESTION 3:   What do you want to know?
   a. *if*
   b. *when*
   c. *what*
   d. *who*

QUESTION 4: What do you wonder?
   a. *why*
   b. *if*
   c. *what*
   d. *who*
   e. *how*
   f. *whether*

14-5   NOUN CLAUSES WHICH BEGIN WITH *THAT*

<table>
<tr>
<td>

    S   **V**   **O**
(a) ⌐I¬ ⌐think¬ ⌐*that Mr. Jones is a good teacher.*¬

(b) I hope *that you can come to the game.*
(c) Mary realizes *that she should study harder.*
(d) I dreamed *that I was on the top of a mountain.*

</td>
<td>

A noun clause can be introduced by the word *that*.
In (a): *that Mr. Jones is a good teacher* is a noun clause. It is the object of the verb *think*.
"*That*-clauses" are frequently used as the objects of verbs which express mental activity. (See the list below.)

</td>
</tr>
<tr>
<td>

(e) I think *that Mr. Jones is a good teacher.*
(f) I think Ø *Mr. Jones is a good teacher.*

</td>
<td>

The word *that* is often omitted, especially in speaking. (e) and (f) have the same meaning.

</td>
</tr>
</table>

COMMON VERBS FOLLOWED BY "*THAT*-CLAUSES"★

assume that	*guess that*	*learn that*	*realize that*
believe that	*hear that*	*notice that*	*suppose that*
discover that	*hope that*	*predict that*	*suspect that*
dream that	*know that*	*prove that*	*think that*

★The verbs in the above list are those that are emphasized in the exercises. Some other common verbs that can be followed by "*that*-clauses" are:

agree that	*fear that*	*imagine that*	*read that*	*reveal that*
conclude that	*feel that*	*indicate that*	*recall that*	*show that*
decide that	*figure out that*	*observe that*	*recognize that*	*teach that*
demonstrate that	*find out that*	*presume that*	*regret that*	*understand that*
doubt that	*forget that*	*pretend that*	*remember that*	

Complete the sentences with the clauses in the list or with your own words. Use *that* to introduce the clause, or omit *that* if you wish.

> *All people are equal.*
> *Flying in an airplane is safer than riding in a car.*
> *He always twirls his mustache when he's nervous.*
> *High school students in the United States don't study as hard as the students in my country do.*
> *A huge monster was chasing me.*
> *I should study tonight.*
> *I will get married someday.*
> ✓ *I will have a peanut butter sandwich.*
> *John "Cat Man" Smith stole Mrs. Adams's jewelry.*
> *More than half of the people in the world go hungry every day.*
> *People are pretty much the same everywhere.*
> *Plastic trash kills thousands of marine animals every year.*

1. I'm hungry. I guess ___**(that) I will have a peanut butter sandwich.**___

2. I have a test tomorrow. I suppose _____,
   but I'd rather go to a movie.

3. Why are you afraid to fly in an airplane? Read this report. It proves

   _____

4. Right now I'm single. I can't predict my future exactly, but I assume

   _____

5. Last night I had a bad dream. In fact, it was a nightmare. I dreamed

   _____

6. The police are investigating the burglary. They don't have much
   evidence, but they suspect _____

7. My cousin feels that people in the United States are unfriendly, but I
   disagree with him. I've discovered _____

8. I've learned many things about life in the United States since I came
   here. For example, I've learned _____

9. I always know when Paul is nervous. Have you ever noticed

   _____

10. I believe that it is wrong to judge another person on the basis of race,
    religion, or sex. I believe _____

11. World hunger is a serious problem. Do you realize _____

_____

12. Don't throw that plastic bag into the sea! Don't you know _____

_____

□ **EXERCISE 15—WRITTEN:** Complete the following sentences with your own words. Omit the word *that* if you wish. (Use your own paper.)

1. I believe that . . . .
2. I assume that . . . .
3. Do you realize that . . . ?
4. I can prove that . . . .
5. I predict that . . . .
6. I've heard that . . . .
7. I guess that . . . .
8. I suppose that . . . .
9. Have you ever noticed that . . . ?
10. I suspect that . . . .
11. I hope that . . . .
12. Do you think that . . . ?
13. I've discovered that . . . .
14. Did you know that . . . ?
15. Last night I dreamed that . . . .

14-6 SUBSTITUTING *SO* FOR A *"THAT*-CLAUSE" IN CONVERSATIONAL RESPONSES

(a) A: Is Pedro from Mexico? B: **I think so**. (*I think **that Pedro is from Mexico**.*) (b) A: Does Judy live in Dallas? B: **I believe so**. (*I believe **that Judy lives in Dallas**.*) (c) A: Did you pass the test? B: **I hope so**. (*I hope **that I passed the test**.*)	***Think**, **believe**,* and ***hope*** are frequently followed by *so* in conversational English in response to a yes/no question. They are alternatives to answering *yes*, *no*, or *I don't know*.★ ***So*** replaces a "*that*-clause." In (a): *so* = *that Pedro is from Mexico*.
(d) A: Is Ali at home? B: **I don't think so**. (*I don't think **that Ali is at home**.*) (e) A: Is Jack married? B: **I don't believe so**. (*I don't believe **that Jack is married**.*)	Negative usage of ***think so*** and ***believe so***: *I don't think so.* *I don't believe so.*
(f) A: Did you fail the test? B: **I hope not**. (*I hope **that I didn't fail the test**.*)	Negative usage of ***hope*** in conversational responses: *I hope not.*

★In addition to expressions with ***think, believe,*** and ***hope,*** the following expressions are commonly used in conversational responses: *I guess so, I guess not, I suppose so, I suppose not, I'm afraid so, I'm afraid not.*

☐ **EXERCISE 16—ORAL:** Give the full idea of SPEAKER B's answers to A's questions by using a "*that*-clause."

1. A: Is Karen going to be home tonight?

   B: I think so. → *I think that Karen is going to be home tonight.*

2. A: Is the library open on Sunday evenings?

   B: I believe so.

3. A: Does Ann speak Spanish?

   B: I don't think so.

4. A: Are we going to have a test in grammar tomorrow?

   B: I don't believe so.

5. A: Will Tina be at the conference in March?

   B: I hope so.

6. A: Will your flight be canceled because of the bad weather in Denver?

   B: I hope not.

☐ **EXERCISE 17—ORAL (BOOKS CLOSED):** Answer the questions by using *think so* or *believe so* if you are not sure, or *yes* or *no* if you are sure.

> *Example:* Does this book have more than (400) pages?
> *Response:* I think/believe so. OR: I don't think/don't believe so. OR: Yes, it does. OR: No, it doesn't.

1. Does (. . .) have a car?
2. Are we going to have a test tomorrow?
3. Is there a fire extinguisher in this building?
4. Is Chicago farther north than New York City?
5. Does the word "patient" have more than one meaning?
6. Does the word "dozen" have more than one meaning?
7. Is your left foot bigger than your right foot?
8. Do gorillas eat meat?
9. Do spiders have eyes?
10. Don't look at your watch. Is it (10:45) yet?
11. Is the nearest post office on (Pine Street)?
12. Is next (Tuesday) the (24th)?
13. Are cats colorblind?
14. Can I buy a window fan at (*name of a local store*)?

15. Can you jog (five miles) without stopping?
16. Do any English words begin with the letter "x"?
17. In terms of evolution, is a pig related to a horse?
18. Is a tomato a vegetable?
19. Have I asked you more than 20 questions in this exercise?
20. Do you know what a noun clause is?
21. Is (...) planning to get married soon?
22. Does (...) usually use chopsticks when s/he eats at home?

14-7   OTHER USES OF "*THAT*-CLAUSES"

(a) I'm **sure that** the bus stops here. (b) I'm **glad that** you're feeling better today. (c) I'm **sorry that** I missed class yesterday. (d) I **was disappointed that** the peace conference failed.	"*That*-clauses" can follow certain expressions with **be** + *adjective* or **be** + *past participle*. The word "*that*" can be omitted with no change in meaning: *I'm sure Ø the bus stops here.*
(e) **It is true that** the world is round. (f) **It is a fact that** the world is round.	Two very common expressions followed by "*that*-clauses" are: *it is true (that)* *it is a fact (that)*

COMMON EXPRESSIONS FOLLOWED BY "*THAT*-CLAUSES"★

be afraid that	*be disappointed that*	*be sorry that*	*It is true that* ...
be aware that	*be glad that*	*be sure that*	*It is a fact that* ...
be certain that	*be happy that*	*be surprised that*	
be convinced that	*be pleased that*	*be worried that*	

★The above list contains expressions emphasized in the exercises. Some other common
expressions with **be** that are frequently followed by "*that*-clauses" are:

be amazed that	*be delighted that*	*be impressed that*	*be sad that*
be angry that	*be fortunate that*	*be lucky that*	*be shocked that*
be ashamed that	*be furious that*	*be positive that*	*be terrified that*
be astounded that	*be horrified that*	*be proud that*	*be thrilled that*

☐ **EXERCISE 18—ORAL:** Complete the sentences. Use any appropriate verb form in the "*that*-clause." (Notice the various verb forms used in the example.) Omit *that* if you wish.

Example: I'm glad that ....

Responses: I'm glad that {
the weather is nice today.
I passed the test.
Sam is going to finish school.
I've already finished my homework.
I can speak English.

1. I'm pleased that . . . .
2. I'm sure that . . . .
3. I'm surprised that . . . .
4. Are you certain that . . . ?
5. I'm very happy that . . . .
6. I'm sorry that . . . .
7. I'm not sorry that . . . .

8. I'm afraid that . . . .*
9. Are you aware that . . . ?
10. I'm disappointed that . . . .
11. I'm convinced that . . . .
12. It is true that . . . .
13. It is a fact that . . . .
14. It's not true that . . . .

☐ **EXERCISE 19—WRITTEN:** Complete the following with your own words. Use noun clauses. (Use your own paper.)

1. I feel that . . . .
2. I regret that . . . .
3. I wonder if . . . .
4. You are lucky that . . . .
5. I'm delighted that . . . .
6. Do you know where . . . ?
7. I doubt that . . . .
8. I can't remember what . . . .
9. It is a fact that . . . .

10. The little boy is ashamed that . . . .
11. I'm amazed that . . . .
12. Do you know whether . . . ?
13. I want to know why . . . .
14. My friend and I agree that . . . .
15. I'm worried that . . . .
16. Are you certain that . . . ?
17. I don't know when . . . .
18. I don't know if . . . .

☐ **EXERCISE 20—ORAL (BOOKS CLOSED)** Review separable phrasal verbs by completing the sentences with pronouns and prepositions.

Example: I wanted to be sure to remember (. . .)'s phone number, so I wrote . . . .

Response: it down.

1. I can't hear the tape. Could you please turn . . . ?
2. I have an application form for (*name of a school*). I have to fill . . . .
3. I dropped my book. Could you please pick . . . ?
4. This is a hard problem. I can't figure . . . .
5. I bought these shoes a few days ago. Before I bought them, I tried . . . .
6. Where's your homework? Did you hand . . . ?

---

*Sometimes **be afraid** expresses fear:
  I don't want to go near that dog. I'm afraid that it will bite me.
Sometimes **be afraid** expresses polite regret:
  I'm afraid you have the wrong number. = I'm sorry, but I think you have the wrong number.
  I'm afraid I can't come to your party. = I'm sorry, but I can't come to your party.

7. (...) asked (...) to go to a movie with him. He asked ....
8. We postponed the picnic. We put ....
9. I misspelled a word on my composition, so I crossed ....
10. I didn't know the meaning of a word, so I looked ....
11. We don't need that light. Would you please turn ...?
12. My coat was too warm to wear inside, so I took ....
13. That music is too loud. Could you please turn ...?
14. These papers are for the class. Could you please hand ...?
15. (...) was going to have a party, but s/he canceled it. S/he called ....
16. I was thirsty, but my glass was empty. So I filled ....
17. My coat is in the closet. I hung ....
18. The story I told wasn't true. I made ....
19. When I wrote a check, I made a mistake. So I tore ....
20. I was cold. So I reached for my sweater and put ....
21. (...) fell asleep in class, so I woke ....
22. I was finished with the tools, so I put ....
23. I don't need these papers, so I'm going to throw ....
24. Let's listen to the radio. Would you please turn ...?

CHAPTER 15
Quoted Speech and Reported Speech

15-1 QUOTED SPEECH

Sometimes we want to quote a speaker's words—to write a speaker's exact words. Exact quotations are used in many kinds of writing, such as newspaper articles, stories and novels, and academic papers. When we quote a speaker's words, we use quotation marks.

SPEAKER: SPEAKER'S EXACT WORDS	QUOTING THE SPEAKER'S WORDS
Jane: *Cats are fun to watch.*	(a) Jane said, "Cats are fun to watch."
Mike: *Yes, I agree. They're graceful and playful. Do you own a cat?*	(b) Mike said, "Yes, I agree. They're graceful and playful. Do you own a cat?"

HOW TO WRITE QUOTATIONS:
1. Put a comma after *said.*★ —————————▶ Jane said,
2. Put quotation marks. —————————————▶ Jane said, "
3. Capitalize the first word of the quotation. ——▶ Jane said, "C
4. Write the quotation. Put a final period. ———▶ Jane said, "Cats are fun to watch.
5. Put quotation marks *after* the period. ————▶ Jane said, "Cats are fun to watch."

6. When there are two (or more) sentences in a quotation, put the quotation marks at the beginning and end of the whole quote. Do not put quotation marks around each sentence.	Mike said, "Yes, I agree. They're graceful and playful. Do you own a cat?"
7. As with a period, put the quotation marks after a question mark at the end of a quote.	INCORRECT: Mike said, "Yes, I agree." "They're graceful and playful." "Do you own a cat"?

8. Be sure to put quotation marks above the line, not on the line.

   INCORRECT: *Ann said, „My book is on the table.„*

   CORRECT: *Ann said, "My book is on the table."*

★Other common verbs besides *say* that introduce quotations: *admit, announce, answer, ask, complain, explain, inquire, report, reply, shout, state, write.*

☐ **EXERCISE 1:** Write sentences in which you quote the speaker's exact words. Use *said*. Punctuate carefully.

1. ANN: My sister is a student.

_____ ***Ann said, "My sister is a student."*** _____

2. JENNIFER: We're hungry.

_____

3. JENNIFER: We're hungry. Are you hungry, too?

_____

4. JENNIFER: We're hungry. Are you hungry, too? Let's eat something.

_____

5. HAMLET: To be or not to be: that is the question.

_____

6. JOHN F. KENNEDY: Ask not what your country can do for you. Ask what you can do for your country.

_____

_____

7. THE FOX: I'm going to eat you.*

_____

   THE RABBIT: You have to catch me first!

_____

_____

---

*In folk tales, animals are frequently given the ability to speak.

□ **EXERCISE 2—ORAL/WRITTEN (BOOKS CLOSED):** Practice writing quoted speech.

1. Write exactly what I say. Identify that I said it. Punctuate carefully.
   a. (Say one short sentence—e.g., *The weather is nice today.*)
   b. (Say two short sentences—e.g., *The weather is nice today. It's warm.*)
   c. (Say two short sentences and one question—e.g., *The weather is nice today. It's warm. Do you like warm weather?*)
2. Write exactly what your classmates say.
   a. (. . .), please say one short sentence.
   b. (. . .), please ask one short question.
   c. (. . .), please say one short sentence and ask one short question.
3. (. . .) and I are going to have a short conversation. Everyone should write exactly what we say.
4. Pair up with another student. Have a brief conversation. Then write your conversation using quoted speech.

□ **EXERCISE 3—WRITTEN:** Write a composition. Choose one of the following topics.

Topic 1: Write a folk tale from your country in which animals speak. Use quotation marks.

Topic 2: Write a children's story that you learned when you were young. When the characters in your story speak, use quotation marks.

Topic 3: Make up a children's story or any kind of story. When the characters in your story speak, use quotation marks.

Topic 4: Write a joke in which at least two people are talking to each other. Use quotation marks when the people are speaking.

Topic 5: Make up an interview you would like to have with a famous person. Use your imagination. Write the imaginary interview using quotation marks.

15-2 QUOTED SPEECH vs. REPORTED SPEECH★

QUOTED SPEECH:	*Quoted speech* refers to reproducing another person's exact words. Quotation marks are used.
REPORTED SPEECH:	*Reported speech* refers to reproducing the idea of another person's words. Not all of the exact words are used: verb forms and pronouns may change. Quotation marks are not used.

QUOTED SPEECH	**REPORTED SPEECH**	Notice in the examples: The verb forms and pronouns change from quoted speech to reported speech.
(a) Ann said, **"I am hungry."**	(b) Ann said **that she was hungry.**	
(c) Tom said, **"I need my pen."**	(d) Tom said **that he needed his pen**.	

★*Quoted speech* is also called *direct speech*. *Reported speech* is also called *indirect speech*.

15-3 VERB FORM USAGE IN REPORTED SPEECH: FORMAL SEQUENCE OF TENSES

FORMAL:	If the main verb of the sentence is in the past (e.g., *said*), the verb in the noun clause is usually also in a past form.* Notice the verb form changes in the examples below.

QUOTED SPEECH	REPORTED SPEECH
(a) He said, "I *work* hard." ⟶	He said (that) he *worked* hard.
(b) He said, "I *am working* hard." ⟶	He said (that) he *was working* hard.
(c) He said, "I *have worked* hard." ⟶	He said (that) he *had worked* hard.
(d) He said, "I *worked* hard." ⟶	He said (that) he *had worked* hard.
(e) He said, "I *am going to work* hard." ⟶	He said (that) he *was going to work* hard.
(f) He said, "I *will work* hard." ⟶	He said (that) he *would work* hard.
(g) He said, "I *can work* hard." ⟶	He said (that) he *could work* hard.
(h) He said, "I *may work* hard." ⟶	He said (that) he *might work* hard.
(i) He said, "I *have to work* hard." ⟶	He said (that) he *had to work* hard.
(j) He said, "I *must work* hard." ⟶	He said (that) he *had to work* hard.
(k) He said, "I *should work* hard." ⟶	He said (that) he *should work* hard. (*no change*)
(l) He said, "I *ought to work* hard." ⟶	He said (that) he *ought to work* hard. (*no change*)

INFORMAL:	Sometimes, especially in speaking, the verb in the noun clause is not changed if the speaker is reporting something *immediately* or *soon after* it was said.

(m) Immediate reporting:	A:	What did Ann just say? I didn't hear her.
	B:	She *said* (that) she *is* hungry.
(n) Later reporting:	A:	What did Ann say when she got home last night?
	B:	She *said* (that) she *was* hungry.

*If the main verb of the sentence is in the present (e.g., *says*), no change is made in the verb tense or modal in the noun clause.

He says, "I *work* hard." ⟶ He says (that) he *works* hard.
He says, "I*'m working* hard." ⟶ He says (that) he*'s working* hard.
He says, "I *worked* hard." ⟶ He says (that) he *worked* hard.
He says, "I *will work* hard." ⟶ He says (that) he *will work* hard.

□ **EXERCISE 4:** Change the quoted speech to reported speech. Change the verb in quoted speech to a past form in reported speech as appropriate.

1. Jim said, "I am sleepy." _____ *Jim said (that) he was sleepy.* _____

2. Sally said, "I don't like chocolate." _____

3. Mary said, "I am planning to take a trip." _____

4. Tom said, "I have already eaten lunch." _____

5. Kate said, "I called my doctor." _____

6. Mr. Rice said, "I'm going to go to Chicago." _____

7. Eric said, "I will come to the meeting." _____

8. Jean said, "I can't afford to buy a new car." _____

9. Jessica said, "I may go to the library." _____

10. Ted said, "I have to finish my work." _____

11. Ms. Young said, "I must talk to Professor Reed." _____

12. Alice said, "I should visit my aunt and uncle." _____

15-4 USING *SAY* vs. *TELL*

(a) Ann *said that* she was hungry.	*Say* is followed immediately by a noun clause.
(b) Ann *told me that* she was hungry. (c) Ann *told us that* she was hungry. (d) Ann *told John that* she was hungry. (e) Ann *told someone that* she was hungry.	*Tell* is NOT followed immediately by a noun clause. *Tell* is followed immediately by a (pro)noun object (e.g., *me, us, John, someone*) and then by a noun clause. INCORRECT: Ann told that she was hungry.

☐ **EXERCISE 5—ORAL:** Practice using *told (someone)* in reported speech.

Example: I need to talk to you.
STUDENT A: (*With book open, choose a sentence at random and whisper to B.*)
I need to talk to you.
STUDENT B: (*With book closed, report to the group.*)
(Ali) **told me** that he needed to talk to me.★

I will call you tomorrow.	I walked to school this morning.
I know your cousin.	I have to take another English course.
I have met your roommate.	I think you speak English very well.
I'm getting hungry.	You should see (*title of a movie*).
I'm not married.	I'll meet you after class for a cup of coffee.
I like your (*shirt/blouse*).	I'm going to take a vacation in (*Hawaii*).
I won't be in class tomorrow.	Your pronunciation is very good.
I can't read your handwriting.	I've already seen (*title of a movie*).
I don't like (*a kind of food*).	I may be absent from class tomorrow.

_____

★In immediate reporting, it is not necessary to change the noun clause verb to a past form.
You may wish to practice both forms:
  Immediate reporting, informal: *(Ali) told me that he **needs** to talk to me.*
  Formal sequence of tenses: *(Ali) told me that he **needed** to talk to me.*
NOTE: In spoken English and in informal written English, sometimes native speakers change noun clause verbs to past forms and sometimes they don't.

☐ **EXERCISE 6—ORAL (BOOKS CLOSED):** Practice reporting a writer's words.

STUDENT A: Write one sentence on a piece of paper. Begin your sentence with "I." Sign your name. Hand your paper to STUDENT B.

STUDENT B: Report what STUDENT A has written. Use the verb **wrote** instead of **said.**

Example: (Pablo) writes something on a piece of paper.
Written: **I'm going to have lunch at MacDonald's.**
Reported: (Pablo) wrote that he was (OR: is) going to have lunch at MacDonald's.

15-5 USING *ASK IF*

Ask, NOT **say** or **tell**, is used to report yes/no questions.	
YES/NO QUESTION **NOUN CLAUSE** Sam said to me, *"Are you hungry?"* (a) Sam **asked** me *if I was hungry.* Sam said to Jane, *"Are you hungry?"* (b) Sam **asked** *Jane if she was hungry.*	
(c) INCORRECT: Sam asked me that I was hungry.	**If**, NOT **that**, is used after **ask** to introduce a noun clause.
(d) Sam *asked* me **if** I was hungry. (e) Sam *asked* me **whether** I was hungry.	**Whether** has the same meaning as **if**. (See Chart 14-4 for the use of **or not**.)
(f) Sam **asked if** I was hungry.	The (pro)noun object (e.g., *me*) may be omitted after **ask**.
(g) Sam **wanted to know if** I was hungry. (h) Sam **wondered if** I was hungry. (i) Sam **inquired whether** or not I was hungry.	In addition to **ask**, yes/no questions can be reported by using **want to know**, **wonder**, and **inquire**.

☐ **EXERCISE 7—ORAL:** Practice using *asked if.*

STUDENT A: Say the words in the book to STUDENT B.

STUDENT B: Don't look at your book. Report STUDENT A's question. Use **asked**.

Example: Are you married?
STUDENT A: Are you married?
STUDENT B: (Ali) asked me if I am married. OR: (Ali) asked me if I was married.*

---

*Immediate reporting, informal: *(Ali) asked me if **I'm** married.*
Formal sequence of tenses: *(Ali) asked me if **I was** married.*

1. Do you know my cousin?
2. Are you hungry?
3. Can you speak (French)?
4. Did you enjoy your vacation?
5. Are you going to take another English course?
6. Will you be at home tonight?
7. Have you ever been in (Mexico)?
8. Can you hear me?
9. Are you listening to me?
10. Do you need any help?
11. Did you finish your homework?
12. Do you think it's going to rain?
13. Are you going to go downtown tomorrow?
14. Do you know how to cook?
15. Do you know whether or not (. . .) is married?
16. Can you come to my party?
17. Do you have a car?
18. Have you ever been in (Russia)?
19. Did you move into a new apartment?
20. Are you going to call me tonight?

□ **EXERCISE 8—ORAL:** Practice using noun clauses after *asked.*★

STUDENT A: Say the words in the book to STUDENT B.
STUDENT B: Don't look at your book. Report STUDENT A's question. Use *asked.*

Example: Where do you live?
STUDENT A: Where do you live?
STUDENT B: (Maria) asked me where I live. OR: (Maria) asked me where I lived.

1. Where is your apartment?
2. Is your apartment far from here?
3. What do you need?
4. Do you need a pen?
5. When does the semester end?
6. Does the semester end in (December)?
7. Why is (. . .) absent?
8. Is (. . .) absent?
9. How often do you go downtown?
10. Do you go downtown every week?

★See 14-2 for the use of question words in noun clauses.

□ **EXERCISE 9:** Complete the sentences by changing the quoted speech to reported speech. Practice using the formal sequence of tenses.

1. Bob said, "Where do you live?"

   Bob asked me _____ ***where I lived.*** _____

2. He said, "Do you live in the dorm?"

   He asked me _____

3. I said, "I have my own apartment."

   I told him _____

4. He said, "I'm looking for a new apartment."

   He said _____

5. He said, "I don't like living in the dorm."

   He told me _____

6. I said, "Do you want to move in with me?"

   I asked him _____

7. He said, "Where is your apartment?"

   He asked me _____

8. I said, "I live on Seventh Avenue."

   I told him _____

9. He said, "I can't move until the end of the semester."

   He said _____

10. He said, "I will cancel my dorm contract at the end of the semester."

    He told me _____

11. He said, "Is that okay?"

    He asked me _____

12. I said, "I'm looking forward to having you as a roommate."

    I told him _____

□ **EXERCISE 10:** Change the reported speech to quotations. Use quotation marks.

1. Eric asked me if I had ever gone skydiving.

   Eric said ___ , ***"Have you ever gone skydiving?"*** ___

2. Chris wanted to know if I would be at the meeting.

   Chris said _____

3. Kate wondered whether I was going to quit my job.

Kate said _____

4. Anna asked her friend where his car was.

Anna said _____

5. Brian asked me what I had done after class yesterday.

Brian said _____

6. Luigi asked me if I knew Italian.

Luigi said _____

7. Debra wanted to know if I could guess what she had in her pocket.

Debra asked _____

8. My boss wanted to know why I wasn't working at my desk and why I
was wasting the company's time.

My boss angrily asked me _____

☐ **EXERCISE 11:** Complete the sentences by changing the sentences in quotation marks to
noun clauses. Practice using the formal sequence of tenses.

1. *"Where do you live?"* Tom asked me . . . ***where I lived.***

2. *"Do you live in the dorm?"* He asked me . . . ***if I lived in the dorm.***

3. *"I stole the money."* The thief admitted . . . ***that he had stolen the money.***

4. *"Where is Jane?"* Ed asked me . . . .

5. *"I'm going to quit school and get a job."* Jessica announced . . . .

6. *"Did you mail the letter?"* Tim asked me . . . .

7. *"What are you thinking about?"* Karen asked me . . . .

8. *"I have to go to the drug store."* Steve said . . . .

9. *"I can't pick you up at the airport."* Alice told me . . . .

10. *"I will take a taxi."* I told her . . . .

11. *"You should speak English as much as possible."* My teacher told me . . . .

12. *"Do you like spaghetti?"* Don asked me . . . .

13. *"Have you already eaten dinner?"* Sue asked me . . . .

14. *"Did you finish your work?"* Jackie asked me . . . .

15. *"What time do you want to leave for the airport?"* Harry asked me . . . .

16. *"I made a mistake."* Carol admitted . . . .

17. *"The final exam will be on the 15th."* The teacher announced . . . .

18. *"An earthquake occurred in Peru."* The newspaper reported . . . .

□ **EXERCISE 12—WRITTEN:** Complete the following. Use the formal sequence of tenses.

1. . . . asked me if . . . .
2. . . . asked me where . . . .
3. . . . told me that . . . .
4. . . . said that . . . .
5. . . . asked me when . . . .
6. . . . told my friend that . . . .
7. . . . asked my friend if . . . .
8. . . . asked my friend why . . . .

□ **EXERCISE 13:** Read the dialogues and complete the sentences. Use the formal sequence of tenses.

1. A: *Oh no! I forgot my briefcase! What am I going to do?*
   B: *I don't know.*

   → When Bill got on the bus, he realized that he ___**had forgotten**___

   his briefcase.

2. A: *Where's your bicycle, Jimmy?*
   B: *I sold it to a friend of mine.*
   A: *You what?*

   → Yesterday I asked my fourteen-year-old son where his bicycle

   _____. He told me that he _____ it to

   a friend of his. I was flabbergasted.

3. A: *Look at this!*
   B: *What?*
   A: *My test paper. I got an "F." I'm sorry I didn't study harder.*

   → When George got his test paper back, he was sorry that he

   _____ harder.

4. A: *The bus is supposed to be here in three minutes. Hurry up! I'm afraid we'll miss it.*
   B: *I'm ready. Let's go.*

   → I told my friend to hurry because I was afraid that we _____

   _____ the bus.

5. A: *Can you swim?*
   B: *Yes.*
   A: *Thank heavens.*

   → When the canoe tipped over, I was glad that my friend _____

   _____.

6. A: *Do you want to go downtown?*
   B: *I can't. I have to study.*

   → When I asked Kathy if she _____ to go downtown,

   she said that she _____ because she _____

   _____.

7. A: *Ow! My finger really hurts! I'm sure I broke it.*
   B: *Let me see.*

   → When Nancy fell down, she was sure that she _____

   her finger.

8. A: *Where's Jack? I'm surprised he isn't here.*
   B: *He went to Chicago to visit his sister.*

   → When I got to the party, I asked my friend where Jack _____.

   I was surprised that he _____ there. My friend told

   me that Jack _____ to Chicago to visit his sister.

9. A: *Will you be home in time for dinner?*
   B: *I'll be home around 5:30.*

   → My wife asked me if I _____ home in time for dinner.

   I told her that I _____ home around 5:30.

10. A: *Have you ever been in Mexico?*
    B: *Yes, I have. Several times.*

    → I asked George if he _____ ever _____ in Mexico. He said

    that he _____ there several times.

15-6 USING VERB + INFINITIVE TO REPORT SPEECH

QUOTED SPEECH	REPORTED SPEECH
(a) Joe said, "Please come to my party."	
(b) Joe said, "Can you come to my party?"	(d) Joe *invited me to come to his party*.
(c) Joe said, "Would you like to come to my party?"	

	S + V + O + INFINITIVE PHRASE	Some verbs are followed immediately by a (pro)noun object and then an infinitive phrase. These verbs (see the list below) are often used to report speech.
(e)	Joe invited me *to come* to his party.	
(f)	I told Ann *to study* harder.	

REPORTING SPEECH: VERB + (PRO)NOUN OBJECT + INFINITIVE★

advise someone to	*invite someone to*	*remind someone to*
ask someone to	*order someone to*	*tell someone to*
encourage someone to	*permit someone to*	*warn someone to*

★Other common verbs followed by a (pro)noun object and an infinitive:

allow	*convince*	*instruct*
beg	*direct*	*persuade*
challenge	*expect*	*urge*

☐ **EXERCISE 14:** Complete each sentence with an infinitive phrase which, combined with the main verb (*invited, advised, etc.*), reports the idea of the speaker's words.

1. Joe said, "Please come to my party."

   Joe invited me _____ ***to come to his party.*** _____

2. My teacher said, "I think you should take another English course."

   My teacher advised me _____ ***to take another English course.*** _____

3. Mrs. Jacobson said, "You may use the phone."

   Mrs. Jacobson permitted me _____

4. The doctor said, "Take a deep breath."

   The doctor told the patient _____

5. My mother said, "Make an appointment with the dentist."

   My mother reminded me _____

6. My friend said, "I think you should take a long vacation."

   My friend encouraged me _____

7. The Smiths said, "Would you like to come to our house for dinner?"

   The Smiths invited us _____

8. My friend said, "You should see a doctor about the pain in your knee."

My friend advised me _____

9. The judge said, "You must pay a fine of fifty dollars."

The judge ordered Mr. Silverman _____

10. Bill said, "Don't touch that hot pot."

Bill warned me _____ ***not to touch that hot pot.***

11. Sue said, "Don't buy a used car."

Sue advised me _____

12. Mr. Gray said, "Don't play in the street."

Mr. Gray warned the children _____

□ **EXERCISE 15:** Following are some dialogues. Report *the first speaker's words*. Use the verb in parentheses and an infinitive phrase.

1. JOE: Would you like to go to a movie with me?
   MARY: Yes.

   (*invite*) _____ ***Joe invited Mary to go to a movie with him.***

2. DR. MILLER: You should get more exercise.
   STEVE: I'll try.

   (*advise*) _____

3. MS. HOLT: Could you please open the door for me?
   TOM: I'd be happy to.

   (*ask*) _____

4. NANCY: Call me around nine.
   ME: Okay.

   (*tell*) _____

5. MR. WARD: You may have a cookie and a glass of milk.
   THE CHILDREN: Thanks, Dad.

   (*permit*) _____

6. PROF. LARSON: You should take a physics course.
   ME: Oh?

   (*encourage*) _____

---

*To make an infinitive negative, put ***not*** in front of it.

7. THE POLICE OFFICER: Put your hands on top of your head!

    THE THIEF: Who? Me? I didn't do anything!

    (*order*) _____

    _____

8. JACK: Don't worry about me.

    HIS MOTHER: I won't.

    (*tell*) _____

    _____

9. SUE: Don't forget to call me.

    ME: I won't.

    (*remind*)★ _____

10. ALICE: Don't forget to lock the door.

    HER ROOMMATE: Okay.

    (*remind*) _____

11. MRS. PETERSON: Please don't slam the door.

    HER DAUGHTER: Okay, Mom.

    (*ask*) _____

12. PROF. ROTH: Don't look directly at the sun during a solar eclipse.

    US: Okay.

    (*warn*) _____

★Two possible sentences: *Sue reminded me to call her.*
Sue reminded me not to forget to call her.

☐ **EXERCISE 16—ERROR ANALYSIS:** All of the following sentences contain mistakes in grammar. Can you find the mistakes and correct them?

1. She asked me that I wanted to go to the music festival.

2. Tom said me that he was hungry.

3. Bob asked me where do you live.

4. Ann told that she had enjoyed the party.

5. Kathy asked me open the window.

6. My friend told to me that she understood my problem.

7. My mother asked me when am I coming home?

8. Do you know where is the nearest gas station?

9. David invited me for eating dinner with him.

10. I asked Tom that when will your plane arrive?

11. I told Bobby don't pull the cat's tail.

12. Ann said, Are you tired?

15-7 SOME TROUBLESOME VERBS: *ADVISE, SUGGEST,* AND *RECOMMEND*

(a) Ed *advised me **to call*** a doctor. (b) Ed *advised **calling*** a doctor.	(a) and (b) have the same meaning. In (a): When *advise* is followed by a (pro)noun object, an infinitive is used. In (b): When there is no (pro)noun object after *advise*, a gerund is used.
(c) Ed *suggested **calling*** a doctor. (d) Ed *recommended **calling*** a doctor.	*Suggest* and *recommend* can also be followed immediately by a gerund.

(e)   CORRECT: Ed ***suggested that I should call*** a doctor.
    INCORRECT: Ed suggested me to call a doctor.
(f)   CORRECT: Ed ***recommended that I should call*** a doctor.
    INCORRECT: Ed recommended me to call a doctor.
	Suggest and *recommend* cannot be followed by a (pro)noun object and an infinitive, but they can be followed by a "*that*-clause" in which *should* is used.*

*The use of *should* in the noun clause is not necessary. However, if *should* is not used, the verb in the noun clause is always in the simple form after *suggest* and *recommend:*

Ed *suggested/recommended* that
⎧ ***I call*** a doctor. (not *called*)
⎨ ***we call*** a doctor. (not *called*)
⎪ ***Ann call*** a doctor. (not *calls* or *called*)
⎩ ***he call*** a doctor. (not *calls* or *called*)

☐ **EXERCISE 17:** Complete the sentences. Give the idea of the speaker's words.

1. The doctor said to me, "You should lose weight."
   a. The doctor advised me _____*to lose weight.*_____
   b. The doctor advised _____*losing weight.*_____
   c. The doctor suggested _____
   d. The doctor recommended _____
   e. The doctor suggested that _____
   f. The doctor recommended that _____

2. My teacher said, "You should study harder."
   a. My teacher suggested that _____
   b. My teacher advised me _____
   c. My teacher advised _____
   d. My teacher recommended _____

3. Mr. Madison said, "Why don't you buy a motorcycle?"
   Mr. Madison suggested _____

4. Don said, "I think you should see a doctor about that problem."
   Don recommended _____

5. Mary said, "Let's go to a movie."
   Mary suggested _____

6. Sharon said, "I think you should go to Iowa State University."
   Sharon advised _____

☐ **EXERCISE 18:** Work in pairs. Each pair should create a short dialogue (five to ten sentences) based on one of the given situations. Each pair will then present their dialogue to the class. After the dialogue, the class will report what was said.

Sample situation: Have a conversation about going somewhere in this city.

Sample dialogue:
ANN: Would you like to go to the zoo tomorrow?
BOB: I can't. I have to study.
ANN: That's too bad. Are you sure you can't go? It will take only a few hours.
BOB: Well, maybe I can study in the morning and then go to the zoo in the afternoon.

ANN: Great! What time do you want to go?

BOB: Let's go around two o'clock.

Sample report:

Ann asked Bob if he wanted to go to the zoo tomorrow. Bob said that he could not go because he had to study. Ann finally persuaded him to go. She said that it would take only a few hours. Bob decided that he could study in the morning and go to the zoo in the afternoon. Ann asked Bob what time he wanted to go. He suggested going around two o'clock.

(Notice in the sample report: The writer gives the idea of the speakers' words without necessarily using the speakers' exact words.)

1. Have a conversation in which one of you invites the other one to a party.

2. One of you is a teenager and the other one is a parent. The teenager is having problems at school and is seeking advice and encouragement.

3. The two of you are a married couple. One of you is reminding the other one about the things s/he should or has to do today.

4. Have a conversation in which one of you persuades the other one to begin a health program by taking up a new kind of exercise (jogging, walking, tennis, etc.). Beginning of the dialogue:

    A: I need to get some physical exercise.
    B: Why don't you take up . . . ?
    A: No, I don't want to do that.

5. One of you is fourteen years old and the other is the parent. The fourteen-year-old wants to say out late tonight. What will the parent say?

6. One of you is a store detective and the other is a shoplifter. The store detective has just seen the shoplifter take something.

7. One of you is a stubborn, old-fashioned, uneducated person who thinks the world is flat. The other one tries to convince the stubborn one that the world is round.

CHAPTER **16**

Using Wish; *Using* If

16-1 EXPRESSING WISHES ABOUT THE PRESENT/FUTURE

THE TRUE SITUATION	EXPRESSING A WISH ABOUT THAT SITUATION	People often make wishes when they want reality to be different, to be exactly the opposite of (contrary to) the true situation.
I *don't know* how to dance.	(a) I *wish* (that) I **knew** how to dance.	
I *don't have* a bicycle.	(b) I *wish* I **had** a bicycle.	A noun clause* usually follows **wish**. Special verb forms are used in the noun clause. When a speaker expresses a wish about a *present* situation, s/he uses a *past* verb form.
Ron *has to work* tonight.	(c) Ron *wishes* he **didn't have to work** tonight.	
I *can't speak* Chinese.	(d) I *wish* I **could speak** Chinese.	
I'm *not* home in bed. Ann *isn't* home in bed. It's cold today. We *aren't* in Hawaii.	(e) I *wish* **I were** home in bed. (f) Ann *wishes* **she were** home in bed. (g) I *wish* **it weren't** cold today. (h) We *wish* **we were** in Hawaii.	Notice in (e), (f), (g), and (h): **were** is used for all subjects: *I wish* { I / you / he / she / it / we / they } **were** . . . .

*For more information about noun clauses which begin with **that,** see Chapter 14.

☐ **EXERCISE 1:** Use the given information to complete the sentences.

THE TRUE SITUATION	EXPRESSING A WISH
1. I don't have a car.	I wish ___*(that) I had a car.*___
2. Alice doesn't have a car.	Alice wishes ___*(that) she had a car.*___
3. I have a cold.	I wish _____
4. I don't have a tape recorder.	I wish _____
5. I don't know how to swim.	I wish _____
6. Bill doesn't have a good job.	Bill wishes _____
7. I live in the dorm.	I wish _____
8. I don't live in an apartment.	I wish _____
9. I can't speak French.	I wish _____
10. Sue can't find a good job.	Sue wishes _____
11. My friend can't come.	I wish _____
12. I'm not at home right now.	I wish _____
13. James isn't here.	I wish _____
14. It isn't Saturday.	I wish _____
15. My friends aren't here.	I wish _____
16. I have to study for a test.	I wish _____
17. I have to write a composition.	I wish _____

☐ **EXERCISE 2—ORAL (BOOKS CLOSED):** Make sentences beginning with "*I wish* ...."

Example: You don't have a bicycle.
Response: I wish (that) I had a bicycle.

1. You don't have a car.
2. You don't have a color TV.
3. You can't whistle.
4. You have a headache.
5. (. . .) isn't here today.
6. It isn't (Sunday).
7. You have to study tonight.
8. You have to go to the dentist.
9. You can't speak (*language*).
10. You can't go to (*place*).
11. You don't have a window fan.
12. You're sleepy.
13. You don't know how to dance.
14. You don't know how to play chess.
15. It's (hot/cold) today.
16. You don't have enough money to buy (a car).
17. You have to work tonight.
18. You can't go to (the zoo) today.
19. You're not rich and famous.
20. You're not in (*country*) right now.

☐ **EXERCISE 3:** Study the examples and then complete the sentences with auxiliary verbs.

  1. I don't have a car, but I wish I _____**did**_____.

  2. I have to study tonight, but I wish I _____**didn't**_____.

  3. I can't speak Italian, but I wish I _____**could**_____.

  4. I'm not tall, but I wish I _____**were**_____.

  5. Alan is tall, but he wishes he _____**weren't**_____.

  6. I don't know Mary Morningstar, but I wish I _____.

  7. I have to take a history course, but I wish I _____.

  8. I can't dance very well, but I wish I _____.

  9. I'm not a good cook, but I wish I _____.

10. Linda isn't a good writer, but she wishes she _____.

11. Jack has to go to the laundromat, but he wishes he _____.

12. Carol doesn't live in the same city as her boyfriend, but she wishes she

      _____.

13. It's too cold to go swimming today, but I wish it _____.

14. Sally can't afford to go to Hawaii, but she wishes she _____.

15. I have to clean my apartment, but I wish I _____.

16. I don't remember that man's name, but I wish I _____.

☐ **EXERCISE 4:** Complete the following conversations. Use auxiliary verbs in the completions.

  1. A: Can you go to the lecture tonight?

     B: No, _____**I can't**_____ , but I wish _____**I could**_____ .

  2. A: Are you a good musician?

     B: No, _____, but I wish _____.

  3. A: Do you smoke?

     B: Yes, _____, but I wish _____.

  4. A: Does your son know how to play a musical instrument?

     B: No, _____, but I wish _____.

  5. A: Can you play a musical instrument?

     B: No, _____, but I wish _____.

6. A: Do you have to take the bus to work?

   B: Yes, _____, but I wish _____.

7. A: Is Maria in your class?

   B: No, _____, but she wishes _____.

8. A: Do you understand what Professor Martin is talking about?

   B: No, _____, but I wish _____.

9. A: Do you know the people who live in the apartment next to yours?

   B: No, _____, but I wish _____.

10. A: Is your roommate neat?

    B: No, _____, but I wish _____.

11. A: Are the students always on time for class?

    B: No, _____, but the teacher wishes _____.

12. A: Do you have enough time to drink a cup of coffee between classes?

    B: No, _____, but I wish _____.

13. A: Can you come over to my house for dinner tomorrow night?

    B: I'm sorry, but we _____. We wish _____.

14. A: Is there a grocery store near your apartment?

    B: No, _____, but I wish _____.

15. A: Is there an art museum in this town?

    B: No, _____, but I wish _____.

16-2 EXPRESSING WISHES ABOUT THE PAST

The PAST PERFECT* is used after *wish* when people make wishes about a past situation.	
THE TRUE SITUATION	**MAKING A WISH ABOUT THE PAST**
I *didn't study* for the test.	(a) *I wish* (that) I ***had studied*** for the test.
Jim *didn't finish* his work.	(b) *Jim wishes* he ***had finished*** his work.
I *went* to the meeting.	(c) *I wish* I ***hadn't gone*** to the meeting.

*See Chart 7-10 for the forms of the past perfect.

☐ **EXERCISE 5:** Use the given information to make sentences with *wish*.

THE TRUE SITUATION	MAKING A WISH
1. Bobby didn't tell me the truth.	I wish **(that) Bobby had told me the truth.**
2. I didn't call my friend last night.	I wish _____
3. I didn't cash a check yesterday.	I wish _____
4. Tom spent all of his money yesterday.	Tom wishes _____
5. I didn't go to class yesterday.	I wish _____
6. Anna didn't finish high school.	Anna wishes _____
7. Jerry wasn't at the meeting last week.	I wish _____
8. Jerry isn't here today.	I wish _____
9. Emily doesn't understand my problem.	I wish _____
10. Emily didn't help me.	I wish _____

☐ **EXERCISE 6:** Complete the sentences with the correct form of the words in parentheses.

1. It took me three days to get to Chicago by bus. I wish I (*fly*) _____ _____ there instead of taking the bus.

2. I miss my family. I wish they (*be*) _____ here now.

3. The kitchen is a mess this morning. I wish I (*wash*) _____ the dishes last night.

4. I'd like to wear my black suit to the meeting today, but it's wrinkled and dirty. I wish I (*take*) _____ it to the cleaner's last week.

5. I have to walk up three flights of stairs to get to my apartment. I wish my apartment building (*have*) _____ an elevator.

6. I wish I (*know*) _____ more English.

7. Sue bought a used car a couple of months ago. It's given her nothing but trouble. She wishes she (*buy, not*) _____ it.

8. I'm tired today. I wish I (*stay up, not*) _____ late last night.

9. I'd like to go camping this weekend. I wish the weather (*be, not*) _____ so cold.

10. I wish I (*can remember*) _____ where I put the
pliers. I can't find them anywhere.

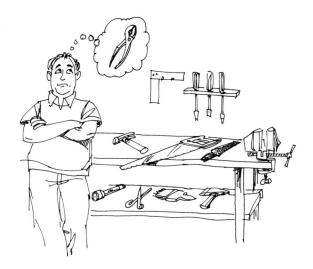

11. You told me to save a little money out of each of my paychecks, but I
didn't. I wish I (*take*) _____ your advice.

12. My brother goes to school in another city. He came here last Friday to
spend a few days with me. I've enjoyed having him here. I wish he
(*have to leave, not*) _____ today. I wish he (*can
spend*) _____ a few more days here.

□ **EXERCISE 7:** Complete the sentences with auxiliary verbs.

1. Bobby didn't tell me the truth, but I wish he _____**had**_____.

2. I don't know Carol Jones, but I wish I _____**did**_____.

3. I can't move into a new apartment, but I wish I _____.

4. I didn't finish my homework last night, but I wish I _____.

5. Sally didn't come to the party last night, but I wish she _____.

6. I don't have enough money to buy that coat, but I wish I _____.

7. I'm too tired to go for a walk, but I wish I _____.

8. I didn't study any English before I came here, but I wish I _____.

9. Dick doesn't live close to school, but he wishes he _____.

10. Jane can't speak Arabic, but she wishes she _____.

☐ **EXERCISE 8:** Complete the following conversations. Use auxiliary verbs in the completions.

1. A: Did you go to the party last night?

   B: Yes, _____*I did*_____, but I wish _____*I hadn't*_____. It was boring.

2. A: Did you eat breakfast this morning?

   B: No, _____, but I wish _____. I'm hungry. My stomach is growling.

3. A: Do you exercise regularly?

   B: No, _____, but I wish _____. I always feel better when I exercise regularly.

4. A: Did you study for the test?

   B: No, _____, but I wish _____. I got an "F" on it.

5. A: Are you a good artist?

   B: No, _____, but I wish _____. I'd like to be able to draw.

6. A: Did you go to the movie last night?

   B: Yes, _____, but I wish _____. It was a waste of time and money.

7. A: Do you have to eat at the student cafeteria?

   B: Yes, _____, but I wish _____. The food is lousy.

8. A: Can you speak Chinese?

   B: No, _____, but I wish _____.

9. A: Is it hard to learn a second language?

   B: Yes, _____, but I wish _____.

☐ **EXERCISE 9—ORAL (BOOKS CLOSED):** Answer *no*. Use *wish*.

   Example: Can you speak Arabic?
   Response: No, I can't, but I wish I could.

1. Did you study last night?
2. Did you go to bed early last night?
3. Do you have a car?
4. Are you (*a movie star*)?
5. Can you speak (*language*)?
6. Did you eat breakfast?

7. Is (. . .) here today?
8. Do you know how to dance?
9. Did (. . .) call you last night?
10. Can you play (*a musical instrument*)?
11. Are you full of energy today?
12. Do you live in an apartment?
13. Is the weather nice today?
14. Did (. . .) help you with your homework?
15. Is your family here?
16. Do you have to go to class tomorrow?
17. Can you buy (a Rolls Royce)?
18. Do you know how to type?

☐ **EXERCISE 10—ORAL:** Make wishes based on the given situations. Try to think of as many possible wishes as you can for each situation.

Example: You're hungry. What do you wish?
Responses: I wish I'd eaten breakfast.
I wish I had a candy bar.
I wish I could go to (*name of a place*) and get a hamburger.
I wish I weren't in class right now.
I wish I didn't have to go to another class after this one.
I wish the classroom were a restaurant and I had a steak in front of me instead of my grammar book.
Etc.

1. You're tired.
2. You're broke.
3. The weather is . . . today.
4. You live in (*kind of residence*).
5. You don't have many talents.
6. This is a nice classroom, but . . . .
7. You're very busy. You have a lot of things to do today.
8. Things about yourself and your life that you would like to change.
9. There are many problems in today's world.

☐ **EXERCISE 11—ORAL (BOOKS CLOSED):** Mention something that is not perfect in your life and then make a wish.

Example: Not everything in your life is perfect. Tell me something that makes you unhappy about your life.
Response: My classes begin at 8 o'clock in the morning.
Teacher: What do you wish?
Response: I wish my classes didn't begin at eight.
I wish my classes began at ten.
I wish I didn't have to get up so early.

*(To the teacher: You may wish to expand the exercise to include an introduction to conditional sentences with **if**.)*

Teacher: What would you do if your classes didn't begin at eight?
Response: If my classes didn't begin at eight, I would sleep until the middle of the morning.

16-3 USING *IF*: CONTRARY-TO-FACT IN THE PRESENT/FUTURE

If is often used to talk about situations that are contrary to fact, i.e., situations that are the opposite of the true situation.

TRUE SITUATION:	(a) I *don't have* enough money.
MAKING A WISH:	(b) I wish I *had* enough money.
USING *IF*:	(c) If I *had* enough money, I *would buy* a car.
	(d) If I *had* enough money, I *could buy* a car.
TRUE SITUATION:	(e) The weather *isn't* nice today.
MAKING A WISH:	(f) I wish the weather *were* nice today.
USING *IF*:	(g) If the weather *were* nice today, I *would go* to the park.
	(h) If the weather *were* nice today, I *could go* to the park.

Contrary-to-fact sentences with an "*if*-clause" and a "result clause" are called *conditional sentences*. Special verb forms are used. The SIMPLE PAST TENSE is used to discuss a present or future situation in an "*if*-clause." **Would** or **could** is used in the result clause.

IF-CLAUSE: simple past tense   **RESULT CLAUSE: *would*/*could* + simple form**

if-clause result clause (i) ⌐If I *had* enough money,⌐ ⌐I *would buy* a car.⌐ result clause *if*-clause (j) ⌐I *would go* to the park⌐ ⌐if the weather *were* nice.⌐	In (i) and (j), the speakers are talking about present/future situations, but they use the simple past in the "*if*-clause."*

(k) If I had enough money, I *would* buy a car.
    (The speaker wants to buy a car.)
(l) If I had enough money, I *could* buy a car.
    (The speaker is expressing a possibility.)
	Would expresses intended or desired results.
	Could expresses possible options.
	Could = *would be able to.*

(m) If the **weather were** nice, I'd go to the park. (n) If **Kate were** here, she would help us. (o) If **I were** you, I wouldn't accept that job.	Notice in (m), (n), and (o): **were** (instead of **was**) is usually used for singular subjects in a contrary-to-fact "*if*-clause."

*An "*if*-clause" is a kind of adverb clause. See Chart 9-6.

☐ **EXERCISE 12:** Complete the sentences with words in parentheses.

1. TRUE SITUATION: I don't have enough time.

   a. I wish I (*have*) _____ enough time.

   b. If I (*have*) _____ enough time, I (*go*) _____
      to the park.

2. TRUE SITUATION: I don't have enough money.

   a. I wish I (*have*) _____ enough money.

   b. If I (*have*) _____ enough money, I (*fly*) _____
      home this weekend.

3. TRUE SITUATION: It's cold today.

   a. I wish it (*be, not*) _____ cold today.

   b. If it (*be, not*) _____ cold today, I (*go*) _____
      swimming.

4. TRUE SITUATION: I don't know how to swim.

   a. I wish I (*know*) _____ how to swim.

   b. If I (*know*) _____ how to swim, I (*go*) _____
      to the beach with you.

5. TRUE SITUATION: I don't understand that sentence.

   a. I wish I (*understand*) _____ that sentence.

   b. If I (*understand*) _____ that sentence, I (*explain*)
      _____ it to you.

6. TRUE SITUATION: I have to go to class today.

   a. I wish I (*have to go, not*) _____ to class
      today.

   b. If I (*have to go, not*) _____ to class today, I
      (*go*) _____ shopping, or I (*visit*) _____
      _____ my friends.

7. TRUE SITUATION: It isn't Saturday.

   a. I wish it (*be*) _____ Saturday.

   b. If it (*be*) _____ Saturday, I (*go*) _____
      to the beach.

8. TRUE SITUATION: I'm not rich.

    a. I wish I (*be*) _____ rich.

    b. If I (*be*) _____ rich, I (*live*) _____ on

       a farm and (*raise*) _____ horses.

☐ **EXERCISE 13:** Complete the sentences with the words in parentheses.

1. Jim doesn't study hard. If he (*study*) _____ **studied** _____ harder,

    he (*get*) _____ **would get** _____ better grades.

2. The weather isn't nice. I (*take*) _____ a walk if the

    weather (*be*) _____ nice.

3. My wife and I want to buy a house, but houses are too expensive. We

    (*buy*) _____ a house if we (*have*) _____

    enough money for a down payment.

4. If money (*grow*) _____ on trees, all of us (*be*) _____ rich.

5. Life (*be*) _____ boring if everyone (*have*)

    _____ the same opinions about everything.

6. If I (*be*) _____ you, I (*tell*) _____ Brian

    the truth.

7. Airplane tickets are expensive. If they (*be*) _____ cheap, I

    (*fly*) _____ to Singapore for the weekend.

8. I wish I (*have*) _____ a camera. I (*take*) _____

    a picture of the sunset tonight if I (*have*) _____ a camera.

9. The student cafeteria is relatively inexpensive, but the food isn't very

    good. I (*eat*) _____ there all the time if the food

    (*be*) _____ better.

10. Sometimes our teacher gives surprise quizzes. If I (*teach*) _____

    this English class, I (*give, not*) _____ surprise

    quizzes.

11. I wish I (*have*) _____ a car. If I (*have*) _____ a car, I

    (*drive*) _____ to school.

12. I'm very tired tonight. If I (*be, not*) _____ tired, I (*go*)

    _____ to the movie with you.

□ **EXERCISE 14—ORAL (BOOKS CLOSED):** *What would you do if you were... ?* Practice using verb forms in contrary-to-fact sentences with *if*.

Example: (What would you do if you were) a house painter?
Response: If I were a house painter, I would (paint houses, paint your house, etc.).

Example: a cat
Response: If I were a cat, I would (chase mice, jump into your lap, etc.).

1. a bird
2. a mountain climber
3. an artist
4. a secretary
5. a dog
6. a good cook
7. a teacher
8. a police officer
9. a parent
10. hungry

11. sleepy
12. at home
13. (. . .)
14. (*name of a famous person*)
15. a professional athlete
16. a surgeon
17. a photographer
18. a mouse
19. (*name of a world leader*)
20. the leader of your country

21. a magician
22. an astronaut
23. ninety years old
24. at/in (*a particular place*)
25. a genius
26. a billionaire
27. the captain of a ship
28. ambitious

16-4 USING *IF*: TRUE vs. CONTRARY-TO-FACT IN THE PRESENT/FUTURE

TRUE SITUATION: (a) If you **need** some money, I $\left\{ \begin{array}{c} will \\ can \end{array} \right\}$ lend you some. (*simple present*)	In (a): Perhaps you need some money. If that is true, I will (or can) lend you some. Reminder: Do not use **will** in an "*if*-clause." (See Chart 3-5.)
CONTRARY-TO-FACT SITUATION: (b) If you **needed** some money, I $\left\{ \begin{array}{c} would \\ could \end{array} \right\}$ lend you some. (*simple past*)	In (b): In truth, you don't need any money. But if the opposite were true, I would (or could) lend you some.

VERB FORM USAGE SUMMARY (PRESENT/FUTURE)

SITUATION:	*IF*-CLAUSE:	RESULT CLAUSE:
TRUE	**simple present**	$\left\{ \begin{array}{c} will \\ can \end{array} \right\}$ + **simple form**
CONTRARY-TO-FACT	**simple past**	$\left\{ \begin{array}{c} would \\ could \end{array} \right\}$ + **simple form**

□ **EXERCISE 15:** Complete the sentences with the words in parentheses. Some of the sentences express true situations, and some of the sentences express contrary-to-fact situations.

1. Maybe I will have enough time tonight. If I (*have*) _____**have**_____ enough time, I (*write*) _____**will write**_____ a letter to my cousin.

2. I won't have enough time tonight. But if I (*have*) _____**had**_____ enough time, I (*write*) _____**would write**_____ a letter to my cousin.

3. Maybe I will have enough money. If I (*have*) _____ enough money, I (*buy*) _____ a ticket to the rock concert.

4. Unfortunately, I don't have enough money. But if I (*have*) _____ enough money, I (*buy*) _____ a ticket to the rock concert.

5. Maybe I will buy a car. If I (*buy*) _____ a car, I (*drive*) _____ to Springfield next month to visit my friend.

6. I'm not going to buy a car. But, if I (*buy*) _____ a car, I (*drive*) _____ to Springfield next month to visit my friend.

7. The weather is terrible today. But if the weather (*be*) _____ good, I (*go*) _____ for a five-mile walk.

8. Maybe the weather will be nice tomorrow. If the weather (*be*) _____ nice, I (*go*) _____ for a long walk.

9. I know that you don't want to go to a movie tonight. But if you (*want*) _____ to go to a movie, I (*go*) _____ with you.

10. What would you like to do tonight? Do you want to go to a movie? If you (*want*) _____ to go to a movie, I (*go*) _____ with you.

□ **EXERCISE 16:** Complete the following with your own words.

1. If I have enough money, _____

2. If I had enough money, _____

3. If I have enough time, _____

4. If I had enough time, _____

5. If the weather is nice tomorrow, _____

6. If the weather were nice today, _____

7. If you studied hard, _____

8. If you study hard, _____

9. If my uncle comes to visit me, _____

10. If my uncle were here, _____

11. I would fly to London if _____

12. I will fly to London if _____

13. You would get angry if _____

14. I will get angry if _____

15. I won't be in class tomorrow if _____

16. If I didn't have to go to class tomorrow, _____

16-5 USING *IF*: CONTRARY-TO-FACT IN THE PAST

Conditional sentences that discuss past time have special verb forms:
***If*-CLAUSE: the past perfect   RESULT CLAUSE: *would have/could have* + past participle**

TRUE SITUATION:	(a) I *didn't have* enough money.
MAKING A WISH:	(b) I wish I *had had* enough money.
USING **IF**:	(c) If I ***had had*** enough money, I ***would have bought*** a car.
	(d) If I ***had had*** enough money, I ***could have bought*** a car.
TRUE SITUATION:	(e) The weather *wasn't* nice yesterday.
MAKING A WISH:	(f) I wish the weather *had been* nice yesterday.
USING **IF**:	(g) If the weather ***had been*** nice yesterday, I ***would have gone*** to the park.
	(h) If the weather ***had been*** nice yesterday, I ***could have gone*** to the park.

□ **EXERCISE 17:** Complete the sentences with the words in parentheses.

1. TRUE SITUATION: I didn't have enough time yesterday.

   a. I wish I (*have*) _____ enough time yesterday.

   b. If I (*have*) _____ enough time yesterday. I (*go*)

   _____ to the park.

2. TRUE SITUATION: I didn't have enough money last night.

    a. I wish I (*have*) _____ enough money last night.

    b. If I (*have*) _____ enough money last night, I (*go*)

    _____ to a show.

3. TRUE SITUATION: Mary didn't come to my party last week.

    a. I wish she (*come*) _____ to my party.

    b. If she (*come*) _____ to my party, she (*meet*) _____

    _____ my fiancé.

4. TRUE SITUATION: It was cold yesterday.

    a. I wish it (*be, not*) _____ cold yesterday.

    b. If it (*be, not*) _____ cold yesterday, I (*go*) _____

    _____ swimming.

5. TRUE SITUATION: Jack didn't study for the test.

    a. Jack wishes he (*study*) _____ for the test.

    b. If he (*study*) _____ for the test, he (*pass*)

    _____ it.

16-6   SUMMARY: VERB FORMS IN SENTENCES WITH *IF* (CONDITIONAL SENTENCES)

SITUATION	*IF*-CLAUSE	RESULT CLAUSE	EXAMPLES
TRUE IN THE PRESENT/FUTURE	simple present	*will* / *can* } + simple form	If I *have* enough money, I { *will buy* / *can buy* } a ticket.
CONTRARY-TO-FACT IN THE PRESENT/FUTURE	simple past	*would* / *could* } + simple form	If I *had* enough money, I { *would buy* / *could buy* } a ticket.
CONTRARY-TO-FACT IN THE PAST	past perfect	*would have* / *could have* } + past participle	If I *had had* enough money, I { *would have bought* / *could have bought* } a ticket.

☐ **EXERCISE 18:** Complete the sentences with the words in parentheses.

1. I didn't feel good yesterday. If I (*feel*) _____ better, I
   (*come*) _____ to class yesterday.

2. I don't feel good today. If I (*feel*) _____ better, I (*take*)
   _____ a walk in the park today.

3. I have a cold today, but I will probably feel better tomorrow. If I (*feel*)
   _____ better tomorrow, I (*go*) _____ to
   class.

4. I'm sorry that you didn't come to the party. If you (*come*) _____
   _____, you (*have*) _____ a good time.

5. I didn't know that Bob was sick. If I (*know*) _____ that
   he was sick, I (*take*) _____ him some chicken
   soup.

6. I'm tired. If I (*be, not*) _____ tired, I (*help*) _____
   you.

7. Snow is predicted for tomorrow. If it (*snow*) _____ tomorrow,
   I (*stay*) _____ home.

8. I may have a dollar. Let me look in my wallet. If I (*have*) _____
   a dollar, I (*lend*) _____ it to you.

9. I don't have any money. If I (*have*) _____ a dollar, I (*lend*)
   _____ it to you.

10. I didn't have a dollar yesterday. If I (*have*) _____ a dollar
    yesterday, I (*lend*) _____ it to you.

11. I didn't know it was your birthday yesterday. I wish you (*tell*)
    _____ me. I (*get*) _____ you a
    present if I (*know*) _____ it was your birthday
    yesterday.

12. Why didn't you tell me when your plane was supposed to arrive? If you
    (*tell*) _____ me, I (*pick*) _____
    you up at the airport.

□ **EXERCISE 19—ORAL:** Make sentences with *wish* and *if*. Follow the patterns in the examples.

> *Example:* I don't have enough time.
> *Response:* I wish I had enough time. If I had enough time, I (would/could go shopping this afternoon, etc.).

> *Example:* I didn't have enough time.
> *Response:* I wish I had had enough time. If I'd had enough time, I (would have/could have gone shopping yesterday afternoon, etc.).

1. I don't have enough money.
2. I didn't have enough money.
3. I don't have enough time.
4. I didn't have enough time.
5. The weather isn't nice.
6. The weather wasn't nice.
7. I'm in class right now.
8. I came to class yesterday.
9. My friend isn't at home.
10. My friend wasn't at home.
11. I don't know how to play the guitar.
12. I didn't know that my uncle was in the hospital.

□ **EXERCISE 20—ORAL:** Make sentences with *if*. Follow the patterns in the examples.

> *Example:* If I have enough money, ...
> STUDENT A: If I have enough money, I'll buy (can buy) a car.
> STUDENT B: If I buy a car, I'll drive (can drive) to Florida.
> STUDENT C: If I drive to Florida, I'll go (can go) to Miami.
> STUDENT D: If I go to Miami, I . . . .

> *Example:* If I had enough money, ...
> STUDENT A: If I had enough money, I would buy (could buy) a car.
> STUDENT B: If I bought a car, I would drive (could drive) to Florida.
> STUDENT C: If I drove to Florida, I would go (could go) to Miami.
> STUDENT D: If I went to Miami, I . . . .

> *Example:* If I had had enough money, ...
> STUDENT A: If I had had enough money, I would have bought (could have bought) a car.
> STUDENT B: If I had bought a car, I would have driven (could have driven) to Florida.
> STUDENT C: If I had driven to Florida, I would have gone (could have gone) to Miami.
> STUDENT D: If I had gone to Miami, I . . . .

1. If I have enough money, ...
2. If I had enough money, ...
3. If I had had enough money, ...
4. If I have enough time, ...
5. If I had enough time, ...
6. If I had had enough time, ...
7. If the weather is hot/cold tomorrow, ...
8. If the weather were hot/cold, ...
9. If the weather had been hot/cold yesterday, ...
10. If I had a million dollars, ...

☐ **EXERCISE 21—ORAL (BOOKS CLOSED):** Answer the questions in complete sentences.

1. Where would you be right now if you weren't in class?
2. What would you have done yesterday if you hadn't come to class?
3. What would you do today if you had enough time?
4. What would you have done yesterday if you had had enough time?
5. What would you buy if you had enough money?
6. What would you have bought yesterday if you had had enough money?
7. What would you do if there were a fire in this building?
8. If you had your own private plane, where would you go for dinner tonight?
9. (. . .) is tired today. Give him/her some advice. What would you do if you were (. . .)?
10. (. . .) wants to learn English as quickly as possible. What would you do if you were (. . .)?
11. Could ships sail around the world if the earth were flat?
12. What would happen if there were a nuclear war?
13. What would you do if you were the teacher of this class?
14. Tell me one thing that you did yesterday. What would have happened if you had not (done that)?
15. What would you do tonight if you didn't have to study?
16. What do you wish were different about the world we live in?

☐ **EXERCISE 22—WRITTEN:** Write on the following topic.

In what ways do you wish the world were different? Why do you wish these things? What would be the results?

Preposition Combinations

A   *be* absent from
    be accustomed to
      add *(this)* to *(that)*
    be acquainted with
      admire *(someone)* for *(something)*
    be afraid of
      agree with *(someone)* about/on *(something)*
    be angry at/with
      apologize to *(someone)* for *(something)*
      apply to *(a place)* for *(something)*
      approve of
      argue with *(someone)* about *(something)*
      arrive at *(a building, a room)*
      arrive in *(a city, a country)*
      ask *(someone)* about *(something)*
      ask *(someone)* for *(something)*
    be aware of

B   *be* bad for
      believe in
      belong to
    be bored with/by
      borrow *(something)* from *(someone)*

C   *be* clear to
      compare *(this)* to/with *(that)*
      complain to *(someone)* about *(something)*
    be composed of
      concentrate on
      consist of
    be crazy about
    be crowded with

D   depend on/upon *(someone)* for *(something)*
    be dependent on/upon *(someone)* for *(something)*
    be devoted to

be different from
disagree with *(someone)* about *(something)*
be disappointed in
discuss *(something)* with *(someone)*
divide *(this)* into *(that)*
be divorced from
be done with
dream about/of

E *be* engaged to
be equal to
escape from
be excited about
excuse *(someone)* for *(something)*
be exhausted from

F *be* familiar with
forgive *(someone)* for *(something)*
be friendly to/with
be frightened of/by
be full of

G get rid of
be gone from
be good for
graduate from

H happen to
hear about/of
hear from
help *(someone)* with *(something)*
hide *(something)* from *(someone)*
hope for
be hungry for

I insist on
be interested in
introduce *(someone)* to *(someone)*
invite *(someone)* to *(something)*
be involved in

K *be* kind to
know about

L laugh at
listen to
look at
look for
look forward to

M *be* mad at
   be made of
   be married to
      matter to
   be the matter with
      multiply *(this)* by *(that)*

N *be* nice to

O *be* opposed to

P   pay for
   be patient with
   be pleased with
      point at
   be polite to
   be prepared for
      protect *(this)* from *(that)*
   be proud of

Q *be* qualified for

R *be* ready for
   be related to
      rely on/upon
   be responsible for

S *be* satisfied with
   be scared of/by
      search for
      separate *(this)* from *(that)*
   be similar to
   be sorry about *(something)*
   be sorry for *(someone)*
      speak to/with *(someone)* about *(something)*
      stare at
      subtract *(this)* from *(that)*
   be sure of

T   take care of
      talk to/with *(someone)* about *(something)*
      tell *(someone)* about *(something)*
   be terrified of/by
      thank *(someone)* for *(something)*
   be thirsty for
   be tired from
   be tired of
      travel to

W   wait for
      wait on
   be worried about

APPENDIX 2
Phrasal Verbs

This list contains only those phrasal verbs used in the exercises in the text. The verbs with an asterisk (*) are nonseparable. The others are separable. See Charts 9-8 and 9-9 for a discussion of separable and nonseparable phrasal verbs.

A ask out . . . . *ask someone to go on a date*
C call back . . . . *return a telephone call*
　　call off . . . . *cancel*
　　*call on . . . . *ask to speak in class*
　　call up . . . . *make a telephone call*
　　cross out . . . . *draw a line through*
D do over . . . . *do again*
　　*drop in (on) . . . . *visit without calling first or without an invitation*
　　*drop out (of) . . . . *stop attending school*
F figure out . . . . *find the solution to a problem*
　　fill in . . . . *complete a sentence by writing in a blank*
　　fill out . . . . *write information in a form (e.g., an application form)*
　　fill up . . . . *fill completely with gas, water, coffee, etc.*
　　find out . . . . *discover information*
　　*fool around (with) . . . . . *have fun while wasting time*
G *get along (with). . . . . *have a good relationship with*
　　*get back (from) . . . . *return from a trip*
　　*get in . . . . *enter a car, a taxi*
　　*get off. . . . . *leave a bus, an airplane, a train, a subway, a bicycle*
　　*get on. . . . . *enter a bus, an airplane, a train, a subway, a bicycle*
　　*get out (of) . . . . *leave a car, a taxi*
　　*get over . . . . *recover from an illness*
　　*get through (with) . . . . . *finish*
　　give back. . . . . *return something to someone*
　　give up. . . . . *quit doing something or quit trying*
　　*grow up (in) . . . . *become an adult*

H hand in . . . . *give homework, test papers, etc., to a teacher*

hand out . . . . *give something to this person, then that person, then another person, etc.*

hang up . . . . *(1) hang on a hanger or a hook; (2) end a telephone call*

K *keep on . . . . *continue*

L leave out . . . . *omit*

*look out (for) . . . . *be careful*

look up . . . . *look for information in a reference book*

M make up . . . . *invent*

P pay back . . . . *return money to someone*

pick up . . . . *lift*

put away . . . . *put something in its usual or proper place*

put back . . . . *return something to its original place*

put down . . . . *stop holding or carrying*

put off . . . . *postpone*

R *run into . . . . *meet by chance*

*run out (of) . . . . *finish the supply of something*

S shut off . . . . *stop a machine or light, turn off*

start over . . . . *start again*

T take off . . . . *remove clothes from one's body*

tear down . . . . *destroy a building*

tear off . . . . *detach, tear along a dotted or perforated line*

tear out (of) . . . . *remove a piece of paper from a book or notebook*

tear up . . . . *tear into small pieces*

throw away/out . . . . *put in the trash, discard*

try on . . . . *put on clothing to see if it fits*

turn down . . . . *decrease the volume*

turn off . . . . *stop a machine or a light, shut off*

turn on . . . . *start a machine or a light*

turn up . . . . *increase the volume*

W wake up . . . . *stop sleeping*

*watch out (for) . . . . *be careful*

write down . . . . *write a note on a piece of paper*

APPENDIX 3
Guide for Correcting Writing Errors

To the student: Each number represents an area of usage. Your teacher will use these numbers when marking your writing to indicate that you have made an error. Refer to this list to find out what kind of error you have made and then make the necessary correction.

① SINGULAR-PLURAL

He have ① been here for six month. ①
He has been here for six months.

② WORD FORM

I saw a beauty ② picture.
I saw a beautiful picture.

③ WORD CHOICE

She got on ③ the taxi.
She got into the taxi.

④ VERB TENSE

He is ④ here since June.
He has been here since June.

⑤+ ADD A WORD

I want ∧⑤+ go to the zoo.
I want to go to the zoo.

⑤– OMIT A WORD

She entered to⑤– the university.
She entered the university.

⑥ WORD ORDER

I saw five times⑥ that movie.
I saw that movie five times.

⑦ INCOMPLETE SENTENCE

⑦
I went to bed. Because I was tired.
I went to bed because I was tired.

⑧ SPELLING

⑧
An accident occured.
An accident occurred.

⑨ PUNCTUATION

⑨
What did he say.
What did he say?

⑩ CAPITALIZATION

⑩
I am studying english.
I am studying English.

⑪ ARTICLE

⑪
I had a accident.
I had an accident.

⑫? MEANING NOT CLEAR

⑫?
He borrowed some smoke.
(? ? ?)

⑬ RUN-ON SENTENCE★

⑬
My roommate was sleeping, we didn't
   want to wake her up.
My roommate was sleeping. We didn't
   want to wake her up.

★A run-on sentence occurs when two sentences are incorrectly connected: the end of one sentence and the beginning of the next sentence are not properly marked by a period and a capital letter. (See Chart 9-1.)

Basic Vocabulary List

The following list contains approximately 750 of the most commonly used words in English. *Fundamentals of English Grammar* assumes that students using this book are familiar with most of the words on the list.

The text uses many other words that are not on the list. Students may wish to add new vocabulary to this list.

The list is divided into two groups. Group One contains the most frequently used words. Group Two has other common words that the students will encounter in the text.

The words are listed according to their usual usage: NOUN, VERB, ADJECTIVE, or ADVERB.

BASIC VOCABULARY LIST: GROUP ONE

NOUNS (Group One)

accident	body	country
address	book	cup
afternoon	box	date
age	boy	daughter
air	bread	day
airplane	breakfast	desk
animal	brother	dictionary
apartment	building	dinner
arm	bus	direction
aunt	car	doctor
baby	chair	door
back	child	ear
bank	circle	earth
bed	city	end
beginning	class	evening
bicycle	clothes	eye
bird	coat	face
birthday	color★	family
boat	corner	father

★British English = colour

finger	movie	trouble
fire	music	uncle
fish	name	university
floor	night	vacation
food	noon	vegetable
foot	nose	vocabulary
friend	notebook	voice
front	number	wall
fruit	office	water
future	page	way
garden	parents	weather
glass	park	week
girl	part	wife
hair	party	window
half	past	woman
hand	pen	word
hat	pencil	work
head	people	world
holiday	pepper	year
home	person	zoo
homework	picture	
hospital	place	
hotel	plant	VERBS (Group One)
hour	present	answer
house	price	arrive
human being	problem	ask
husband	question	be
idea	reason	become
information	restaurant	begin
insect	rice	believe
job	river	break
juice	room	bring
land	roommate	build
language	school	buy
leg	shoe	call
letter	side	carry
library	sister	catch
life	sky	change
light	smile	close
line	son	come
lunch	sound	continue
man	street	cost
meat	student	cry
mile	sun	cut
minute	table	die
mistake	teacher	do
money	test	drink
month	thing	eat
moon	time	end
morning	town	enter
mother	tree	explain

fall
feel
fight
find
finish
fix
get
give
go
grow
happen
have
hear
help
hold
hope
hurt
interest
keep
know
laugh
learn
leave
let
like
listen
live
look
lose
love
make
mean
meet
move
need
open
pay
plan
put
rain
read
ride
run
say
see
sell
send
sit
sleep
speak
stand

start
stay
stop
study
take
talk
teach
tell
think
touch
try
turn
use
wait
walk
want
wash
watch
work
write
understand
visit

ADJECTIVES (Group One): Opposites

bad	good
beautiful	ugly
big	little
big	small
cheap	expensive
clean	dirty
cold	hot
cool	warm
dangerous	safe
dark	light
deep	shallow
different	same
difficult	simple
dry	wet
early	late
east	west
empty	full
fast	slow
fat	thin
first	last
happy	sad
hard	easy
hard	soft
healthy	ill
healthy	sick
heavy	light
high	low
intelligent	stupid
large	little
large	small
long	short
messy	neat
modern	old-fashioned
narrow	wide
noisy	quiet
north	south
old	new
old	young
poor	rich
private	public
right	left
right	wrong
rough	smooth
short	tall
sour	sweet
strong	weak

ADVERBS (Group One)

again
ago
also
always
early
ever
fast
finally
generally
hard
here
immediately
late
maybe
never
now
occasionally
often
once

BASIC VOCABULARY LIST: GROUP TWO

NOUNS (Group Two)

amount	game
army	gas(oline)**
art	gold
bag	government
ball	grass
beach	group
bill	hall
blood	health
bottom	heart
bridge	heat
business	hill
cat	history
ceiling	hole
center*	horse
century	hundred
chance	ice
clock	individual
cloud	industry
coffee	island
college	key
computer	kitchen
concert	knife
condition	lake
conversation	law
course	list
crowd	luck
definition	magazine
difference	mail
distance	market
dog	math(ematics)
dress	meaning
earthquake	member
egg	middle
enemy	midnight
example	milk
experience	million
fact	mind
fall/autumn	mountain
fear	mouth
field	nation
flower	nature
forest	neck
form	neighbor
furniture	newspaper

*British English = centre
**British English = petrol

noise
object
ocean
office
opinion
pain
paint
pair
pants
peace
period
picnic
pleasure
pocket
position
power
pronunciation
purpose
radio
result
ring
rule
salt
sandwich
science
sea
season
seat
shape
shirt
shoulder
situation
size
skin
snow
song
space
spelling
spring
stamp
star
store
subject
success
sugar
storm
suit
summer

tape recorder
tea
telephone
television
theater*
thousand
top
toy
train
trip
trouble
umbrella
universe
valley
value
war
wind
wing
winter
wood

VERBS (Group Two)

accept
act
add
agree
allow
appear
attempt
attend
beat
blow
borrow
burn
cause
choose
collect
complete
consider
contain
control
cook
cross
count
cover
dance
decide

disappear
discover
divide
doubt
draw
dream
dress
drive
drop
enjoy
exist
expect
fail
fill
fit
flow
fly
forget
guess
hang
hate
hit
hurry
improve
include
introduce
invite
join
kill
kiss
lead
lend
lift
marry
notice
obtain
offer
order
own
pass
permit
pick
point
pour
practice
prepare
promise
prove

---

*British English = theatre (This spelling is also frequently used in American English.)

provide
pull
push
reach
realize
receive
recognize
refuse
remember
repeat
reply
report
require
return
rise
save
search
seem
separate
serve
share
shout
show
sign
sing
smell
spell
spend
spread
succeed
suggest
supply
surprise
surround
taste
tear
thank
tie
travel
wave
wear
win
wish
wonder
worry

ADJECTIVES (Group Two)

absent
angry
bald
bright
busy
calm
dead
delicious
delightful
dizzy
essential
famous
flat
foolish
foreign
free
fresh
funny
glad
great
handsome
humid
hungry
lazy
mad
native
nervous
nice
pretty
proud
rapid
ripe
round
serious
sharp
sorry
special
strange
terrific
tough
unique
various
whole
wild
wise
wonderful

ADJECTIVE OPPOSITES

accurate	inaccurate
certain	uncertain
clear	unclear
comfortable	uncomfortable
common	uncommon
complete	incomplete
convenient	inconvenient
dependent	independent
direct	indirect
fair	unfair
familiar	unfamiliar
happy	unhappy
healthy	unhealthy
important	unimportant
interesting	uninteresting
kind	unkind
lawful	unlawful
legal	illegal
logical	illogical
necessary	unnecessary
normal	abnormal
pleasant	unpleasant
polite	impolite
possible	impossible
proper	improper
rational	irrational
real	unreal
regular	irregular
responsible	irresponsible
sure	unsure
true	untrue
usual	unusual
visible	invisible

ADVERBS (Group Two)

actually
afterward(s)
almost
already
anymore
anywhere
apparently
carefully
certainly
completely
constantly
downtown
easily
enough
entirely
especially
everywhere
extremely
fortunately
just
later
next
obviously
perhaps
quietly
rarely
regularly
seldom
seriously
somewhere
still
surely
together
too
well
yet

Index—Volume B

Adjective clauses, 309–323 *(Look on pages 309 through 323.)*	The numbers following the words listed in the index refer to page numbers in the main text.
Adjectives: vocabulary list, A10 *(Look in the back part of this book on the tenth page of the Appendixes.)*	Numbers in the index that are preceded by the letter "A" (e.g., A10) refer to pages in the Appendixes, which are found in the last part of the text. The main text ends on page 398, and the Appendixes immediately follow. Page 398 is followed by page A1.
Be afraid, 362 *fn.* *(Look at the footnote on page 362.)*	The letters "*fn.*" mean "footnote." Footnotes are at the bottom of a page or the bottom of a chart.